Tonda L. Hughes
Carrol Smith
Alice Dan
Editors

Mental Health Issues for Sexual Minority Women: Redefining Women's Mental Health

Mental Health Issues for Sexual Minority Women: Redefining Women's Mental Health has been co-published simultaneously as *Journal of Lesbian Studies*, Volume 7, Number 1 2003.

Pre-publication REVIEWS, COMMENTARIES, EVALUATIONS . . .

"MAKES A UNIQUE CONTRIBUTION TO THE LITERATURE in terms of innovative methodologies and addressing gaps in our knowledge base."

Michele J. Eliason, PhD
Associate Professor
University of Iowa

More pre-publication
REVIEWS, COMMENTARIES, EVALUATIONS . . .

Harrington Park Press

Mental Health Issues for Sexual Minority Women: Redefining Women's Mental Health

Mental Health Issues for Sexual Minority Women: Redefining Women's Mental Health has been co-published simultaneously as *Journal of Lesbian Studies*, Volume 7, Number 1 2003.

The *Journal of Lesbian Studies* Monographic "Separates"

Below is a list of "separates," which in serials librarianship means a special issue simultaneously published as a special journal issue or double-issue *and* as a "separate" hardbound monograph. (This is a format which we also call a "DocuSerial.")

"Separates" are published because specialized libraries or professionals may wish to purchase a specific thematic issue by itself in a format which can be separately cataloged and shelved, as opposed to purchasing the journal on an on-going basis. Faculty members may also more easily consider a "separate" for classroom adoption.

"Separates" are carefully classified separately with the major book jobbers so that the journal tie-in can be noted on new book order slips to avoid duplicate purchasing.

You may wish to visit Haworth's website at . . .

http://www.HaworthPress.com

. . . to search our online catalog for complete tables of contents of these separates and related publications.

You may also call 1-800-HAWORTH (outside US/Canada: 607-722-5857), or Fax 1-800-895-0582 (outside US/Canada: 607-771-0012), or e-mail at:

getinfo@haworthpressinc.com

Mental Health Issues for Sexual Minority Women: Redefining Women's Mental Health, edited by Tonda L. Hughes, RN, PhD, FAAN, Carrol Smith, RN, MS and Alice Dan, PhD (Vol. 7, No. 1 2003). *A rare look at mental health issues for lesbians and other sexual minority women.*

Addressing Homophobia and Heterosexism on College Campuses, edited by Elizabeth P. Cramer, PhD (Vol. 6, No. 3/4, 2002). *A practical guide to creating LGBT-supportive environments on college campuses.*

Femme/Butch: New Considerations of the Way We Want to Go, edited by Michelle Gibson and Deborah T. Meem (Vol. 6, No. 2, 2002), *"Disrupts the fictions of heterosexual norms. . . . A much-needed examination of the ways that butch/femme identities subvert both heteronormativity and 'expected' lesbian behavior." (Patti Capel Swartz, PhD, Assistant Professor of English, Kent State University)*

Lesbian Love and Relationships, edited by Suzanna M. Rose, PhD (Vol. 6, No. 1, 2002). *"Suzanna Rose's collection of 13 essays is well suited to prompting serious contemplation and discussion about lesbian lives and how they are–or are not–different from others. . . . Interesting and useful for debunking some myths, confirming others, and reaching out into new territories that were previously unexplored." (Lisa Keen, BA, MFA, Senior Political Correspondent, Washington Blade)*

Everyday Mutinies: Funding Lesbian Activism, edited by Nanette K. Gartrell, MD, and Esther D. Rothblum, PhD (Vol. 5, No. 3, 2001). *"Any lesbian who fears she'll never find the money, time, or support for her work can take heart from the resourcefulness and dogged determination of the contributors to this book. Not only do these inspiring stories provide practical tips on making dreams come true, they offer an informal history of lesbian political activism since World War II." (Jane Futcher, MA, Reporter,* Marin Independent Journal, *and author of* Crush, Dream Lover, *and* Promise Not to Tell)

Lesbian Studies in Aotearoa/New Zealand, edited by Alison J. Laurie (Vol. 5, No. 1/2, 2001). *These fascinating studies analyze topics ranging from the gender transgressions of women passing as men in order to work and marry as they wished to the effects of coming out on modern women's health.*

Lesbian Self-Writing: The Embodiment of Experience, edited by Lynda Hall (Vol. 4, No. 4, 2000). *"Probes the intersection of love for words and love for women. . . . Luminous, erotic, evocative." (Beverly Burch, PhD, psychotherapist and author,* Other Women: Lesbian/Bisexual Experience and Psychoanalytic Views of Women *and* On Intimate Terms: The Psychology of Difference in Lesbian Relationships)

'Romancing the Margins'? Lesbian Writing in the 1990s, edited by Gabriele Griffin, PhD (Vol. 4, No. 2, 2000). *Explores lesbian issues through the mediums of books, movies, and poetry and offers readers critical essays that examine current lesbian writing and discuss how recent movements have tried to remove racist and anti-gay themes from literature and movies.*

From Nowhere to Everywhere: Lesbian Geographies, edited by Gill Valentine, PhD (Vol. 4, No. 1, 2000). *"A significant and worthy contribution to the ever growing literature on sexuality and space. . . . A politically significant volume representing the first major collection on lesbian geographies. . . . I will make extensive use of this book in my courses on social and cultural geography and sexuality and space." (Jon Binnie, PhD, Lecturer in Human Geography, Liverpool, John Moores University, United Kingdom)*

Lesbians, Levis and Lipstick: The Meaning of Beauty in Our Lives, edited by Jeanine C. Cogan, PhD, and Joanie M. Erickson (Vol. 3, No. 4, 1999). *Explores lesbian beauty norms and the effects these norms have on lesbian women.*

Lesbian Sex Scandals: Sexual Practices, Identities, and Politics, edited by Dawn Atkins, MA (Vol. 3, No. 3, 1999). *"Grounded in material practices, this collection explores confrontation and coincidence among identity politics, 'scandalous' sexual practices, and queer theory and feminism. . . . It expands notions of lesbian identification and lesbian community." (Maria Pramaggiore, PhD, Assistant Professor, Film Studies, North Carolina State University, Raleigh)*

The Lesbian Polyamory Reader: Open Relationships, Non-Monogamy, and Casual Sex, edited by Marcia Munson and Judith P. Stelboum, PhD (Vol. 3, No. 1/2, 1999). *"Offers reasonable, logical, and persuasive explanations for a style of life I had not seriously considered before. . . . A terrific read." (Beverly Todd, Acquisitions Librarian, Estes Park Public Library, Estes Park, Colorado)*

Living "Difference": Lesbian Perspectives on Work and Family Life, edited by Gillian A. Dunne, PhD (Vol. 2, No. 4, 1998). *"A fascinating, groundbreaking collection. . . . Students and professionals in psychiatry, psychology, sociology, and anthropology will find this work extremely useful and thought provoking." (Nanette K. Gartrell, MD, Associate Clinical Professor of Psychiatry, University of California at San Francisco Medical School)*

Acts of Passion: Sexuality, Gender, and Performance, edited by Nina Rapi, MA, and Maya Chowdhry, MA (Vol. 2, No. 2/3, 1998). *"This significant and impressive publication draws together a diversity of positions, practices, and polemics in relation to postmodern lesbian performance and puts them firmly on the contemporary cultural map." (Lois Keidan, Director of Live Arts, Institute of Contemporary Arts, London, United Kingdom)*

Gateways to Improving Lesbian Health and Health Care: Opening Doors, edited by Christy M. Ponticelli, PhD (Vol. 2, No. 1, 1997). *"An unprecedented collection that goes to the source for powerful and poignant information on the state of lesbian health care." (Jocelyn C. White, MD, Assistant Professor of Medicine, Oregon Health Sciences University; Faculty, Portland Program in General Internal Medicine, Legacy Portland Hospitals, Portland, Oregon)*

Classics in Lesbian Studies, edited by Esther Rothblum, PhD (Vol. 1, No. 1, 1996). *"Brings together a collection of powerful chapters that cross disciplines and offer a broad vision of lesbian lives across race, age, and community." (Michele J. Eliason, PhD, Associate Professor, College of Nursing, The University of Iowa)*

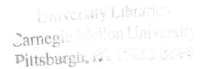

Mental Health Issues for Sexual Minority Women: Redefining Women's Mental Health

Tonda L. Hughes, RN, PhD, FAAN
Carrol Smith, RN, MS
Alice Dan, PhD
Editors

Mental Health Issues for Sexual Minority Women: Redefining Women's Mental Health has been co-published simultaneously as *Journal of Lesbian Studies*, Volume 7, Number 1 2003.

Harrington Park Press
An Imprint of
The Haworth Press, Inc.
New York • London • Oxford

Published by

Harrington Park Press®, 10 Alice Street, Binghamton, NY 13904-1580 USA

Harrington Park Press® is an imprint of The Haworth Press, Inc., 10 Alice Street, Binghamton, NY 13904-1580 USA.

cau

Mental Health Issues for Sexual Minority Women: Redefining Women's Mental Health has been co-published simultaneously as *Journal of Lesbian Studies*™, Volume 7, Number 1 2003.

The development, preparation, and publication of this work has been undertaken with great care. However, the publisher, employees, editors, and agents of The Haworth Press and all imprints of The Haworth Press, Inc., including The Haworth Medical Press® and The Pharmaceutical Products Press®, are not responsible for any errors contained herein or for consequences that may ensue from use of materials or information contained in this work. Opinions expressed by the author(s) are not necessarily those of The Haworth Press, Inc. With regard to case studies, identities and circumstances of individuals discussed herein have been changed to protect confidentiality. Any resemblance to actual persons, living or dead, is entirely coincidental.

Cover design by Lora Wiggins

Library of Congress Cataloging-in-Publication Data

Mental health issues for sexual minority women : redefining women's mental health / Tonda L. Hughes, Carrol Smith, Alice Dan, editors.
        p. cm.
"Mental health issues for sexual minority women: redefining women's mental health has been co-published simultaneously as Journal of lesbian studies, v. 7, no. 1 2003."
Includes bibliographical references and index.
        ISBN 1-56023-310-9 (hbk. : alk. paper) – ISBN 1-56023-311-7 (pbk. : alk. paper)
        1. Minority lesbians–Mental health. 2. Lesbians–Mental health. 3. Bisexual women–Mental health. I. Hughes, Tonda L. II. Smith, Carrol, MSN. III. Dan, Alice J. IV. Journal of lesbian studies.
RC451.4.G39 M447 2003
362.2'086'643–dc21
                                                                                                2002153240

Indexing, Abstracting & Website/Internet Coverage

This section provides you with a list of major indexing & abstracting services. That is to say, each service began covering this periodical during the year noted in the right column. Most Websites which are listed below have indicated that they will either post, disseminate, compile, archive, cite or alter their own Website users with research-based content from this work. (This list is as current as the copyright date of this publication.)

(continued)

*Special Bibliographic Notes related to special journal issues
(separates) and indexing/abstracting:*

- indexing/abstracting services in this list will also cover material in any "separate" that is co-published simultaneously with Haworth's special thematic journal issue or DocuSerial. Indexing/abstracting usually covers material at the article/chapter level.
- monographic co-editions are intended for either non-subscribers or libraries which intend to purchase a second copy for their circulating collections.
- monographic co-editions are reported to all jobbers/wholesalers/approval plans. The source journal is listed as the "series" to assist the prevention of duplicate purchasing in the same manner utilized for books-in-series.
- to facilitate user/access services all indexing/abstracting services are encouraged to utilize the co-indexing entry note indicated at the bottom of the first page of each article/chapter/contribution.
- this is intended to assist a library user of any reference tool (whether print, electronic, online, or CD-ROM) to locate the monographic version if the library has purchased this version but not a subscription to the source journal.
- individual articles/chapters in any Haworth publication are also available through the Haworth Document Delivery Service (HDDS).

Mental Health Issues for Sexual Minority Women: Redefining Women's Mental Health

CONTENTS

ABOUT THE EDITORS

Tonda L. Hughes, RN, PhD, FAAN, is Associate Professor of Nursing and Director of Research for the Center of Excellence in Women's Health at the University of Illinois at Chicago. Dr. Hughes' teaching and research has focused on women's mental health and substance abuse, with a particular focus on lesbians, including risk and protective factors for alcohol abuse in lesbians. She provided expert testimony to the Institute of Medicine's Committee on Lesbian Health Research and was a contributor to the 1999 report of the IOM's findings and recommendations. Dr. Hughes has served as a consultant/advisor to a number of federal agencies, including the National Institute on Alcohol Abuse and Alcoholism (NIAAA), the Centers for Disease Control, Center for Substance Abuse Prevention, Center for Substance Abuse Treatment, and the Office of Research on Women's Health.

Carrol Smith, RN, MS, has worked for many years as a specialist in Women's Health Nursing. She has been involved in a number of women's health studies since 1994, including the Chicago Women's Health Survey, a community-based study of lesbians in Chicago. She was project coordinator for the University of Illinois at Chicago site of a national Phase II HIV preventative vaccine trial and for an NIH-funded grant aimed at lowering the incidence of STDs in women on the West Side of Chicago. Ms. Smith is focusing on lesbian domestic violence as a student in the UIC's PhD nursing program.

Alice Dan, PhD, is Professor in the College of Nursing and the School of Public Health and Director of the Center for Research on Women and Gender at the University of Illinois at Chicago. She also directs the UIC's National Center of Excellence in Women's Health, which has provided a home for the development of the Midwest Lesbian Health Research Consortium.

Foreword

Research on women's mental health has burgeoned in the past several decades. Prodded by the feminist movement and the women's health movement, social scientists have devoted more attention and energy than ever before to this field of study. This research has done much to help dispel earlier beliefs that women are less psychologically healthy than men. Despite the substantial growth in the field as a whole, however, relatively little attention has been paid to the mental health of lesbians and other sexual minority women. Epidemiological studies focusing on mental health have rarely asked about sexual orientation, and broad-based studies of mental health among sexual minority populations are rare. Further, existing research has focused primarily on lesbians; very few studies have included sufficient numbers of bisexual women to permit separate analyses. Consequently, there remains much speculation about the mental health concerns of lesbians and other sexually minority women.

The 1999 Institute of Medicine's (IOM) report on lesbian health research formally documented the existence of large gaps in knowledge about lesbians' health (Solarz, 1999). The IOM expert panel identified the following three overarching priorities for research on lesbian health:

1. Research is needed to better understand the physical and *mental* health status of lesbians and to determine whether there are health problems for which lesbians are at higher risk as well as conditions for which protective factors operate to reduce risk to health of lesbians.
2. Research is needed to better understand how to define sexual orientation in general and lesbian sexual orientation in particular and to better understand the diversity of the lesbian population.

[Haworth co-indexing entry note]: "Foreword." Hughes, Tonda L. Co-published simultaneously in *Journal of Lesbian Studies* (Harrington Park Press, an imprint of The Haworth Press, Inc.) Vol. 7, No. 1, 2003, pp. xix-xxiv; and: *Mental Health Issues for Sexual Minority Women: Redefining Women's Mental Health* (ed: Tonda L. Hughes, Carrol Smith, and Alice Dan) Harrington Park Press, an imprint of The Haworth Press, Inc., 2003, pp. xiii-xviii. Single or multiple copies of this article are available for a fee from The Haworth Document Delivery Service [1-800-HAWORTH, 9:00 a.m. - 5:00 p.m. (EST). E-mail address: getinfo@haworthpressinc.com].

xiii

3. Research is needed to identify possible barriers to access to mental and physical health care services for lesbians and ways to increase their access to these services.

Regarding bisexual women, the IOM panel concluded that information was insufficient to support the development of specific priorities or recommendations–thus emphasizing the great need for research focusing on this group.

This volume brings together recent work concerning the mental health of lesbians and other sexual minority women. Most of the papers present original research and focus on topics including body image and attitudes toward eating and dieting; relationship satisfaction and conflicts; substance use and sexual victimization; risk factors for psychological distress among African American lesbians; and mental health concerns of sexual minority women who present for treatment. Other papers provide reviews of the literature on traumatic victimization, internalized homophobia, and mental health issues for lesbians with physical disabilities–an area that has received almost no attention in the literature. As a whole, the papers address each of the research priorities as well as several methodological issues and knowledge gaps identified in the IOM report.

Sexual orientation is a complex, multidimensional construct. There is growing consensus that sexual orientation encompasses more than lesbian/gay or heterosexual identity and that adequate assessment of this construct requires multiple measures–at least those that assess identity, behavior, and attraction or desire. Nevertheless, few studies have included sufficient numbers of bisexual women to permit separate analyses, and no studies to date have focused exclusively on this subset of the population. Several papers in this volume include data specific to bisexual women and most discuss how findings may (or may not) be relevant to them. For example, in a research report focusing on sexual identity, sexual behavior, and health risks in young, low-income sexual minority women, Scheer, Parks, McFarland et al. point out that mental health concerns and risk factors appear to differ substantially for women who identify as bisexual compared with those who identify as lesbian. Findings on mental health concerns of women who present for treatment reported by Rogers, Emanuel, and Bradford further illustrate the importance of broad inclusion of sexual minority women when exploring mental health concerns and treatment needs of women.

Among other limitations identified in the IOM report is the lack of random samples and appropriate control or comparison groups in studies of lesbian health. Although the majority of studies included here use nonrandom samples, Scheer and her colleagues report data collected from a probability sample of young, low-income women in California. However, all of the other studies do include a comparison group.

Without a comparison group it is difficult to put findings into a context of overall health risk or make statements about relative risk. Three of the studies in this volume include comparison groups of heterosexual women, two compare bisexual women and lesbians (one of these includes additional comparisons based on gender of sex partners), and one compares lesbians and gay men. Three of the studies–those reported by Matthews et al., Owens et al., and Hughes et al.–used a novel strategy for obtaining heterosexual comparison groups. In these studies lesbians were recruited from communities using multiple sources to obtain as diverse a sample as possible. Each lesbian who participated in the studies (self-administered survey questionnaires or face-to-face interviews) was asked to assist in the recruitment of a heterosexual woman whose work-role closely matched the lesbians' own. Demographic characteristics of the heterosexual samples recruited using this method were remarkably similar to the lesbian samples. Importantly, these studies found smaller differences between lesbian and heterosexual women than those reported in earlier lesbian health studies. For example, Matthews and colleagues found that, contrary to previous research findings, lesbian and heterosexual women in committed relationships differed very little in terms of relationship satisfaction, division of labor, frequency of sexual activity, and use of mental health services for relationship problems. Similarly, although Owens et al. found differences between lesbians and heterosexual women on body mass, body image, and attitudes toward eating and dieting, these differences were modest. Finally, the importance of demographic characteristics such as age, race, and education, is also apparent in the study reported by Luhtanen in which she compares demographically similar groups of lesbian/bisexual women and gay/bisexual men on predictors of psychological well-being. Predictors of all three measures of well-being (self-esteem, depression, and life satisfaction) were similar for women and men in the study. In fact, few gender differences were found on any of the study measures. As authors of the above studies point out, using demographically similar comparison groups increases confidence in differences found–a factor that is especially important when using nonprobability samples.

Researchers are beginning to explore other innovative methods of obtaining comparison groups for studies of lesbian health. For example, in a recent study of lesbians' mental health, Rothblum and Factor (2001) used lesbians' sisters as a comparison group. Consistent with previous research findings, lesbians in this study reported higher levels of education than did their heterosexual sisters. Rothblum and Factor suggest that higher levels of education are associated with lesbians' lower likelihood of being married and having children. Each of these factors (higher levels of education, unmarried status, not having children) likely exerts an important influence on lifestyle behaviors and mental health. For example, lesbians in Rothblum and Factor's study were found to have higher self-esteem than their heterosexual sisters.

Despite consistent findings that lesbians tend to be more highly educated than women in the general population, a fundamental theme emerging from the literature–including the papers in this volume–is the existence of tremendous variability within the lesbian/sexual minority population. This heterogeneity poses formidable theoretical and methodological challenges to researchers. While the criticism leveled at lesbian health research for its inclusion of mostly white, middle-class women is not without merit, an argument can also be made that more research is needed that focuses on homogeneous subgroups within the sexual minority population. Until large-scale national studies that permit comparisons among subgroups of lesbians and bisexual women are more feasible, smaller descriptive studies of particular subgroups can provide important information about risk and protective factors specific to these groups. The studies reported by Luhtanen and by Rogers, Emanuel, and Bradford are examples.

The studies reviewed in this volume highlight a number of important areas in which more research is needed. For example, in the literature review focusing on mental health issues for lesbians with disabilities, O'Toole and Brown describe in poignant detail the dearth of information about this population. While emphasizing the great need for more research, they acknowledge the inherent complexity and difficulty in separating out the intersecting influences on mental health of multiple marginalized statuses. African American sexual minority women are another subgroup about which very little is known. Findings comparing psychological distress in African American lesbians and heterosexual women, reported by Hughes et al., are consistent with findings from studies of mostly white lesbians. For example, lesbians in this study were more likely than their heterosexual counterparts to report suicidal ideation and attempts and more likely to have sought mental health counseling, though these differences were smaller than those reported in many other studies of lesbians' health. Szymanski and Chung review the literature on internalized homophobia and point out the need for more research that examines this construct in lesbian samples. An important question raised by these authors is how the experience of stigma and internalized homophobia may differ for lesbian and bisexual women. Finally, Balsam examines several forms of victimization experienced by lesbian and bisexual women using a cultural victimization framework. She asserts that to understand lesbian and bisexual women's victimization experiences, such experiences must be examined within the context of multiple, intersecting oppressions experienced by these groups, and identifies a number of areas in which more research is needed.

As the IOM report points out, "lesbians are a very diverse group, varying along dimensions of sexual orientation and in terms of demographic characteristics such as socioeconomic status, race and ethnicity, culture, religious background, and age" (Solarz, 1999, p. 157). Although the papers included in this volume address many of these dimensions, we realize that they raise more questions than they answer. However, we view the myriad questions as a sign of progress and hope that they serve to challenge and engage researchers interested in this field of study.

Recently, there have been a number of promising initiatives focusing on improving the health of sexual minority populations. These include:

- The IOM report, *Lesbian Health: Current Assessment and Directions for the Future* (Solarz, 1999), funded by the Office of Research on Women's Health, National Institutes of Health and the Office of Women's Health at the Centers for Disease Control and Prevention.
- The National Institute of Mental Health (NIMH) and the American Psychological Association's two-day workshop "New Approaches to Research on Sexual Orientation, Mental Health, and Substance Abuse."
- *Lesbian, Gay, Bisexual, and Transgender Health: Findings and Concerns.* A white paper funded by the U.S. Health and Human Services Administration (HRSA) (Dean et al., 2000).
- *A Provider's Introduction to Substance Abuse Treatment for Lesbian, Gay, Bisexual, and Transgender Individuals* published by the Substance Abuse and Mental Health Services Administration Center for Substance Abuse Treatment (CSAT) (USDHHS, 2001).
- *Healthy People 2010 Companion Document for Lesbian, Gay, Bisexual, and Transgender (LGBT) Health* (GLMA, 2001).
- Amnesty International (2001). *Crimes of hate, conspiracy of silence–torture and ill treatment based on sexual identity.* London: Amnesty International.

In addition, a number of academic and community-based groups have formed to advocate and support research on lesbian and sexual minority women's health. These include, for example, the Chicago Midwest Lesbian Health Research Consortium and the Lesbian Health Institute at the University of California, San Francisco. Each of these initiatives should help to stimulate further research, prevention, and intervention efforts aimed at improving the health and lives of sexual minority women and men.

Tonda L. Hughes

REFERENCES

Amnesty International. Crimes of hate, conspiracy of silence–torture and ill treatment based on sexual identity. London: Amnesty International (2001). (Available at *www.amnesty.org*)

Dean, L., Meyer, I.H., Robinson, K. et al. (2000). Lesbian, gay, bisexual, and transgender health: Findings and concerns. *Journal of the Gay and Lesbian Medical Association, 4,* 101-151.

Gay and Lesbian Medical Association and LGBT Health Experts (2001). Healthy People 2010 Companion Document for Lesbian, Gay, Bisexual, and Transgender (LGBT) Health. San Francisco, CA: GLMA. (Available at *www.glma.org*)

Rothblum, E.D., & Factor, R. (2001). Lesbians and their sisters as a control group: Demographic and mental health factors, *Psychological Science, 12*(1), 63-69.

Solarz, A. (Ed.). (1999). *Lesbian Health: Current assessment and directions for the future.* Washington, DC: National Academy Press.

US Department of Health and Human Services (2001). *A Provider's Introduction to Substance Abuse Treatment for Lesbian, Gay, Bisexual, and Transgender Individuals,* published by the Substance Abuse and Mental Health Services Administration Center for Substance Abuse Treatment (CSAT). DHHS Publication No. (SMA) 01-3498. Rockville, MD.

Traumatic Victimization in the Lives of Lesbian and Bisexual Women: A Contextual Approach

Kimberly F. Balsam

SUMMARY. This paper takes a contextual approach to understanding traumatic victimization experiences of lesbian and bisexual women over the life span. Expanding on feminist perspectives on violence against women, the concept of "cultural victimization" is used to explore the role of societal homophobia in shaping the experience of victimization for lesbian and bisexual women. An overview of the existing literature on the prevalence and impact of childhood abuse, domestic violence, sexual assault, and hate crimes among this population is provided. The relationship between sexual identity development and trauma is discussed. This article provides a framework for understanding lesbian and bisexual women's victimization, lends insight to clinicians working with lesbian/bisexual survivors, and provides direction for future research. *[Article copies available for a fee from The Haworth Document Delivery Service: 1-800-HAWORTH. E-mail address: <getinfo@haworthpressinc.com> Website: <http://www.HaworthPress.com> © 2003 by The Haworth Press, Inc. All rights reserved.]*

Kimberly F. Balsam, MS, is a doctoral student in the clinical psychology program at the University of Vermont. Her clinical, research and teaching interests focus on the psychology of women, traumatic stress, and lesbian, gay, and bisexual psychology.

Address correspondence to: Kimberly F. Balsam, Department of Psychology, John Dewey Hall, University of Vermont, Burlington, VT 05405 (E-mail: Kimfern@aol.com).

[Haworth co-indexing entry note]: "Traumatic Victimization in the Lives of Lesbian and Bisexual Women: A Contextual Approach." Balsam, Kimberly F. Co-published simultaneously in *Journal of Lesbian Studies* (Harrington Park Press, an imprint of The Haworth Press, Inc.) Vol. 7, No. 1, 2003, pp. 1-14; and: *Mental Health Issues for Sexual Minority Women: Redefining Women's Mental Health* (ed: Tonda L. Hughes, Carrol Smith, and Alice Dan) Harrington Park Press, an imprint of The Haworth Press, Inc., 2003, pp. 1-14. Single or multiple copies of this article are available for a fee from The Haworth Document Delivery Service [1-800-HAWORTH, 9:00 a.m. - 5:00 p.m. (EST). E-mail address: getinfo@haworthpressinc.com].

1

KEYWORDS. Lesbians, bisexuality, trauma, victimization, child abuse, domestic violence, sexual assault, hate crimes, homophobia

Over the past two decades, traumatic experiences have increasingly been recognized as having a significant impact on individuals and communities. In particular, scholars have drawn attention to the widespread problem of victimization experienced by women in their families, intimate relationships, and communities. Increasingly, researchers and clinicians recognize victimization experiences as a crucial factor in understanding women's mental health over the life span. Although we are beginning to develop an understanding of traumatic victimization in the lives of women in general, much less attention has been focused on its role in the lives of lesbian and bisexual women. Few studies on victimization assess sexual orientation, and most assume that participants are heterosexual. Conversely, studies of lesbians and bisexual women have not generally adequately assessed for traumatic victimization. Theoretical and clinical writings on violence against women also tend to view this topic through a heterosexual lens, relegating lesbian and bisexual women's experiences to the margins.

The purpose of this paper is to examine the role of traumatic victimization in the lives of lesbian and bisexual women, with an emphasis on how the sociocultural context creates unique risk and resilience factors for this group of women. Using the concept of "cultural victimization," I will explore the role of societal homophobia in shaping the ways in which trauma is experienced by lesbian and bisexual women. I will draw on theory, research and my clinical experience. The paper is intended to provide a conceptual framework for understanding lesbian and bisexual women's victimization, lend insight to clinicians working with lesbian/bisexual survivors of trauma, and provide direction for future research.

FEMINIST MODELS OF VIOLENCE AGAINST WOMEN

Feminist models of violence against women emphasize that psychological, physical, and sexual abuse experienced by women must be examined and understood in the context of sexism in society. Rather than merely a deviant behavior perpetrated by one individual against another, each individual act of violence is embedded in the sociocultural context of the oppression of women, including women's subordinate political and economic status and gendered expectations for male and female behavior (Koss, Goodman, Browne, Keita, & Russo, 1994; Walker, 1994). Sexism in society also influences the impact of violence on women. Root (1992) coined the term "insidious trauma" to refer to the ongoing traumatic impact of living with oppression. Direct experiences of victimization are experienced by women against a backdrop of devaluation and disempowerment. More recently, studies of violence against women have begun to broaden their focus on the "gendered" context of women's lives to incorporate the multiple contextual factors, such as ethnicity and immigrant status, that influence women's experiences (e.g., Root, 1996; Wyatt, 1992).

LESBIAN AND BISEXUAL WOMEN IN CONTEXT

In addition to the experience of sexism and other oppressions such as racism and classism, lesbian and bisexual women live their lives in the context of homophobia and heterosexism. This context may have consequences for lesbian and bisexual women's mental health and well-being. Neisen (1993) coined the term "cultural victimization" to refer to the impact of living in a heterosexist culture, and likens this experience to the trauma of physical and sexual abuse, explaining how both can lead to shame, negative self-concept, self-destructive behaviors, and a "victim mentality." Similarly, Root's (1992) construct of "insidious trauma" can be applied to the stress of living with homophobia. DiPlacido (1998) used the term "minority stress" to refer to the multidimensional construct of stresses associated with being lesbian, gay, or bisexual. She included in her construct of minority stress such experiences as hate crimes, discrimination, the stress of coming out and/or the stress of self-concealment, and internalized homophobia.

All of these models emphasize the importance of understanding the role of the homophobic context in the lives of lesbian and bisexual women. Heterosexism exerts its influence on the individual, interpersonal, and institutional levels, just as sexism does. For lesbian and bisexual women of color, this effect is magnified, as they experience the "triple jeopardy" of racism, sexism and heterosexism (Greene, 1994). For bisexual women, the effect includes biphobic[1] influences that arise not only in the dominant culture, but also within the lesbian and gay community (Ochs, 1996). If we understand the socio-cultural context as an ongoing, "insidious" traumatic influence, then we must examine its potential influence and interaction with any discrete traumatic event that occurs.

VIOLENCE AGAINST LESBIAN AND BISEXUAL WOMEN: PREVALENCE

The homophobic context may have an impact on lesbian and bisexual women's likelihood of experiencing traumatic victimization over the life span.

While there are many myths and assumptions about risk and protective factors, researchers have only recently begun to examine the prevalence of traumatic experiences among this group of women. A review of this literature reveals several methodological problems. Some of these issues, such as homogeneous samples and unstandardized, subjective measures of victimization, are also found in the literature on victimization among the general population of women (see Russell & Bolen, 2000, for a review). As a result of these issues, the prevalence rates found in both populations vary widely, making comparisons between lesbians and heterosexual women difficult. Furthermore, some studies of lesbians do not assess sexual orientation or do not make distinctions between sexual identity and sexual behavior, leaving questions about who is actually included in the sample. Finally, the existing literature focuses almost exclusively on lesbians, ignoring the possibility that traumatic victimization experiences of bisexual women differ in important ways.

Childhood abuse. There is some indication that lesbians are at higher risk than heterosexual women for verbal and physical abuse in childhood and adolescence, both in their families and in their communities. Tjaden, Thoeness, and Allison (1999), in a large representative sample of women, found that 59.5% of those who reported ever living with a same-sex partner also reported a history of physical assault in childhood, compared to 35.7% of those who had only lived with an opposite-sex partner. This abuse might be specifically related to sexual orientation. For example, Pilkington and D'Augelli (1995), in a survey of gay, lesbian, and bisexual adolescents and young adults, found that 22% of their female participants had been "verbally assaulted" and 18% had been "physically assaulted" by a family member because of their sexual orientation.

A particularly sensitive area of research is the question of the prevalence of childhood sexual abuse among lesbian and bisexual women. Cultural myths suggest that such abuse might "cause" homosexuality in women (Butke, 1995). Empirical studies of childhood sexual abuse among lesbians reveal mixed findings. Studies of lesbian samples have found rates comparable to those found in heterosexual samples (e.g., Descamps, Rothblum, Bradford, & Ryan, 2000; Morris, 1997). Other studies that have included both lesbians and heterosexual women have found higher rates among lesbians (Hughes, Haas, Razzano, Cassidy, & Matthews, 2000; Tjaden et al., 1999).

In reporting higher rates of any type of childhood abuse among lesbians, it is important to consider mediators of this experience, with attention to how the homophobic context shapes the early lives of lesbian and bisexual women. It is possible that earlier coming out and gender-role nonconformity may be associated with greater risk for violence. Harry (1989) found that gay men who reported higher levels of gender nonconformity as a child and earlier same-sex experiences in adolescence also reported higher levels of childhood physical abuse. Although not yet examined in larger studies of women, qualitative work by Hall (1998) suggests that lesbian and bisexual women may also be specifically targeted for abuse as a result of gender-nonconforming appearance and behavior. Furthermore, rejection by family and peers may lead to an increase in behaviors that increase a girl's risk for physical and sexual victimization in adolescence, such as substance abuse and running away from home (Kruks, 1991; Savin-Williams, 1994). On the other hand, these higher rates may partially reflect lesbian and bisexual women's greater willingness to disclose histories of abuse to researchers, due to norms for disclosure within the lesbian, gay, bisexual (LGB) community and higher use of psychotherapy.

Domestic violence. Burke and Follingstad (1999), in a review of the literature on same-sex domestic violence, report findings of prevalence rates ranging from 8.5% to 48% across studies of lesbian samples. These rates are roughly comparable to those found among heterosexual samples. However, many studies neglect to identify the gender of the perpetrator, and may therefore obscure the possibility that domestic violence reported by lesbian and bisexual women may have occurred in past or current relationships with men. For example, Tjaden et al. (1999) found that "same-sex cohabitating" women who reported a history of relationship violence were three times more likely to have been abused by a male partner than a female partner.

Sexual assault. Studies that have included both lesbian and heterosexual samples have found higher rates of sexual assault among lesbians (Duncan, 1990; Moore & Waterman, 1999; Tjaden et al., 1999). In contrast, Descamps et al. (2000), in a large sample of lesbians, found that 15% had been sexually assaulted in adulthood, findings comparable to those from heterosexual samples. In some studies, gender of perpetrator is not assessed, leaving unanswered questions about the sources of relative risk for lesbian and bisexual women. Moore and Waterman (1999) found that lesbians in their study who had been sexually assaulted also reported that the perpetrator was a male date. This suggests that some of the risk to lesbians may occur before coming out. However, this may not always be the case. Brand and Kidd (1986) found that 7% of lesbians reported experiencing a sexual assault by a female partner. No studies have yet been conducted that examine the sexual assault experiences of bisexual women.

Hate crimes. Adult lesbian and bisexual women may be specifically targeted for verbal, physical, and sexual violence based on their sexual orientation, either by strangers or persons known to them. Studies of hate crimes have found that this experience is not uncommon. Bradford and Ryan (1988) found that 52% of lesbians reported that they had been verbally attacked and 6% reported that they had been physically attacked because of their sexual orientation. Herek, Gillis, and Cogan (1999) found that 19% of lesbians and 15% of bisexual women reported at least one incident of physical victimization in their lifetime that they perceived to be related to homophobic bias.

VIOLENCE AGAINST LESBIAN AND BISEXUAL WOMEN: IMPACT

Most of the research on violence against lesbians has focused on prevalence. However, the homophobic context may also influence the impact of victimization on lesbian and bisexual women. One possibility is that the stress of living with homophobia might interact with the stress of a traumatic event. Several studies of women in the general population have found that the experience of multiple traumatic experiences can have a profound impact on mental health. Women who have experienced more than one victimization are at much greater risk for poor psychological outcome than those who have experienced only one victimization (Gidycz, Coble, Latham, & Layman, 1993; Messman-Moore, Long, & Siegfried, 2000). Lesbian and bisexual women, regardless of their victimization history, face cultural victimization by a homophobic society (Neisen, 1993). Experiences of psychological, physical or sexual trauma, then, occur against a backdrop of ongoing, "insidious" trauma (Root, 1992). For some women, the result may be similar to revictimization. Furthermore, lesbians and bisexual women must live with the ongoing threat of hate crime victimization to themselves, their families, and their communities. In some instances, lesbian and bisexual women may be unclear as to whether a victimization experience was indeed related to bias. An individual's perception that a victimization experience was related to sexual orientation, whether or not this was made explicit by the perpetrator, has been linked with particularly deleterious effects on mental health and well-being (Herek et al., 1999). For lesbians and bisexual women of color, there is the intersecting issue of racism and racially motivated hate crimes. Together, these factors suggest that the sociocultural context may put lesbian and bisexual women at heightened risk of psychological problems following trauma.

On the other hand, the results of the few studies that have examined the impact of violence suggest that lesbians experience at least some of the same problems as heterosexual women. For example, Descamps et al. (2000) found that victimization was positively associated with depression, daily stress, and alcohol use. Roberts and Sorensen (1999) found that lesbian victims of childhood sexual abuse reported high rates of eating disorders, anxiety disorders, and suicidality. Perry (1995) found that lesbian and bisexual women with histories of domestic violence reported greater use of alcohol and drugs and higher rates of high-risk sexual behaviors. Hughes, Johnson, and Wilsnack (2001) found that childhood sexual abuse was positively associated with alcohol abuse for both lesbians and heterosexual women. However, adult sexual assault was associated with alcohol abuse only for heterosexual women. More research is needed to examine the multitude of ways in which lesbian and bisexual women are impacted by victimization, and how this impact might be similar or different to the impact on heterosexual women.

Homophobia, in addition to affecting the internal well-being of lesbians and bisexual women, also may shape access to services for victims of trauma. Appropriate services might not be available, such as informed and supportive crisis counseling for a woman who has experienced a hate crime. Services that are available might not be specifically targeted to the needs of lesbian and bisexual victims. For example, therapy groups for adult women who have been sexually abused or assaulted might overlook the specific relationship and sexual issues that are relevant to lesbian and bisexual women. A lesbian or bisexual woman may feel uncomfortable disclosing her sexual orientation in such a group, particularly if any group members express stereotypical beliefs about the causal links between sexual abuse and sexual orientation. Lesbian or bisexual women may not disclose their sexual orientation to service providers out of fear of discrimination or blame, and this lack of disclosure may result in less than adequate care. Bisexual women may face particular challenges in seeking help, as the few services targeted to non-heterosexual women are generally focused on the needs of lesbians (Crane, LaFrance, Leichtling, Nelson, & Silver, 1999).

Another issue is the response of the lesbian/gay/bisexual community to victimization. On the one hand, if a lesbian or bisexual woman is involved with a supportive community, she may experience strong support throughout her healing process. Given the high prevalence rates of violence against women, it is likely that others in this community have had similar experiences and can provide a sense of solidarity. If a woman is in a same-sex relationship, her partner might also have experienced victimization, and might provide empathy and understanding. Weingourt (1998) found that lesbian survivors of childhood sexual abuse reported higher current relationship satisfaction than heterosexual survivors did. A lesbian or bisexual woman may be involved in some way with the feminist movement, and this may assist her in developing a critical analysis of her experiences and empower her to take action on both a personal and political level. Bias-related victimization might elicit particularly supportive reactions from a woman's support network.

On the other hand, the response of the lesbian/gay/bisexual community might not always be useful and supportive. The LGB community has historically denied or minimized the existence of same-sex domestic violence. While there are many probable explanations for this, one possibility is that doing so maintains the image of well-being and avoids perpetuating stereotypes of LGB people as "sick" (Balsam, 2001). Silence creates an environment in which a lesbian victim of domestic violence might not receive adequate support from her community. Furthermore, the emphasis on male violence against women can lead to rigid ideas about perpetrators and victims and promote the stereotype that women are not violent. Women who experienced victimization by a female perpetrator, either in childhood or adulthood, may receive less support from their community than if the perpetrator were male (Butke, 1995). Bisexual women victimized by either men or women may encounter biphobic responses from lesbians when seeking help (Sulis, 1999). And lesbian or bisexual women of color may experience racism within the LGB community as well as homophobia in their ethnic/racial communities as they seek support for victimization experiences.

While lesbians and bisexual women may experience unique risks for poor mental health, it is also likely that their experiences have helped them to develop unique strengths or resiliencies that protect against or moderate the experience of victimization. Living with "cultural victimization" on a daily basis means finding creative strategies for coping. In one study, lesbian and gay adolescents were found to use a wide variety of coping strategies and to use these strategies at higher rates than heterosexual adolescents (Lock & Steiner, 1999). This repertoire of coping strategies might be employed in coping with and recovering from the effects of trauma. Similarly, lesbian and bisexual women often create "families of choice," or strong support systems to combat the stress of living with cultural victimization. These support systems may serve as a buffer against the effects of trauma. Indeed, social support has been shown to be an important moderator of the impact of traumatic experiences in adulthood and childhood (Carlson & Dalenberg, 2000) and more specifically, of the impact of homophobic hate crimes (Otis & Skinner, 1996).

There is also evidence that lesbians use psychotherapy and counseling at higher rates than heterosexual women (Rothblum & Factor, 2001). This may be related to cultural norms within the lesbian community, and to the challenges of coming out and being out in a homophobic society. This use of therapy may have a positive impact on lesbian and bisexual women who have experienced previous trauma, giving them an opportunity to understand and work through their reactions. Furthermore, a lesbian or bisexual woman who experiences a trauma may already be in therapy or may find it more acceptable to seek therapy, providing her with a supportive context in which to heal from the trauma.

TRAUMA AND SEXUAL IDENTITY DEVELOPMENT

One of the unique challenges facing lesbian and bisexual women is to negotiate the process of "coming out." In the context of external and internalized homophobia, the lesbian or bisexual woman is faced with the challenge of forging an identity and a life script that stands apart from her culture's expectations. Various models of sexual identity development have been proposed, suggesting that women progress through a series of "stages" culminating in a healthy, integrated identity. Indeed, the degree to which a woman is "out" appears to be related to her mental health and well-being (Morris, Waldo, & Rothblum, 2001). Recent research suggests, however, that there may be a great deal of individual variation in how women experience this process. To some extent, coming out appears to be shaped by contextual factors in a woman's life, such as her race/ethnicity (Morris et al., 2001) or her motherhood status (Balsam, Morris, & Rothblum, 2000). An important issue to consider is how the coming out process might be affected by experiences of victimization, and how, in turn, coming out might shape the impact of victimization on the individual.

On the one hand, coming out might facilitate healing from the impact of trauma. The process of coming out and developing an identity as a lesbian or bisexual woman can be associated with a sense of empowerment and self-efficacy. If one of the effects of traumatic victimization is a sense of powerlessness, then the process of coming out might provide an experience of reclaiming one's personal power. Identifying as a lesbian or bisexual woman means attending to and valuing one's own thoughts and feelings, even when these feelings conflict with cultural expectations and norms. For a survivor of trauma who may have learned to dissociate or "numb out," paying attention to her inner experience can be a powerful aspect of her recovery.

On the other hand, a woman who has experienced traumatic victimization might experience more difficulties in the coming out process. Growing up in a violent home may lead an adolescent to delay coming out due to fear of provoking further violence from family members (Hunter, 1990). In adulthood, the shame and self-doubt associated with trauma might make a woman less likely to trust her own feelings, and she may question whether her feelings of attraction to women are "real" or valid (Hall, 1998). She may have coped with the trauma by dissociating from her feelings, making self-awareness of same-sex thoughts and feelings difficult. This might be particularly true for survivors of sexual abuse. In the face of cultural myths about sexual abuse "causing" sexual orientation, a woman might believe that her same-sex attractions are merely a "symptom" of abuse she experienced by men. Bisexual women might internalize biphobic messages about being "confused" and might blame this on the abuse. On a cognitive level, a survivor of childhood trauma might hold beliefs that she is "bad" and that she does not deserve to be happy, therefore denying herself the opportunity to pursue same-sex relationships. Even if she does, she may feel less well-equipped to face the threat of interpersonal and societal rejection if she comes out publicly.

The degree to which a woman is at risk of certain types of traumatic experiences might be influenced by the degree to which she is out. For example, a lesbian who is closeted at work and in her neighborhood may be at lower risk for homophobic hate crimes perpetrated by acquaintances or strangers. On the other hand, she may be more vulnerable to domestic violence in her intimate relationships, or less likely to get help if she does experience domestic violence by a female partner. If she is not connected to the lesbian community, she may feel that her options for partners are limited, and may be reluctant to leave an abusive relationship. She may be unable to seek help in the face of intimate violence out of fear of disclosing her orientation. Her partner might use this fear as a tool of coercion, threatening to "out" her if she leaves the relationship. Thus, it is likely that being "out" is associated with risks in some areas, and protective factors in other areas.

CONCLUSIONS AND RECOMMENDATIONS

This paper addresses the unique factors related to the prevalence and impact of traumatic victimization experiences in the lives of lesbian and bisexual women. In order to understand these experiences, we must examine them in the context of the multiple, intersecting oppressions experienced by lesbian and bisexual women, and the risk and resilience factors that result from living with cultural victimization. Furthermore, we must not lose sight of the strengths that develop as a result of negotiating the coming out process. For clinicians and other service providers who work with lesbian and bisexual victims of trauma, it is important to be informed about issues related to trauma and sexual orientation, but also to keep an open mind and to hear each woman's unique experience. Understanding a woman's degree of outness, self-identification, level of social support, experiences with discrimination and hate crimes, and integration within the LGB community will help providers identify potential strengths and vulnerabilities. While taking care to avoid perpetuating stereotypes and myths about sexual orientation and victimization, providers should also be willing to explore the ways in which these myths and stereotypes might have influenced the woman's own reactions and/or the reactions of others around them. And finally, it is crucial for providers to also address race, class, religion, and disability in order to fully understand the context of victimization.

Many of the ideas presented here are based on clinical experience and await empirical investigation. It will be important for researchers examining these ideas to overcome the methodological limitations of previous research in order to provide a solid empirical basis for understanding these complex and multifaceted issues. More specifically, it is recommended that researchers use measures of victimization and its sequelae that are standardized and include behavioral indices. Measuring sexual orientation as a multifaceted construct, including identity, behavior, and degree of participation in the LGB community, is similarly important. Large samples of ethnically and geographically diverse women will allow examination of the intersection of multiple contextual factors in women's lives. In particular, it will be important to specifically recruit bisexual women for participation in research, and to ask questions that will capture their unique experiences. Finally, including comparison groups of heterosexual women will be important to understand the unique risks and resiliencies of lesbian and bisexual women.

NOTE

1. Ochs (1996) defines biphobia as the "discrimination, hostility, and invalidation" (p. 217) experienced by bisexuals in both the lesbian/gay and heterosexual communities. Biphobia also includes "the denial of the very existence of bisexual people" (p. 224).

REFERENCES

Balsam, K. F. (2001). Nowhere to hide: Lesbian battering, homophobia, and minority stress. *Women & Therapy, 23*, 25-37.
Balsam, K. F., Morris, J. F., & Rothblum, E. D. (2000, August). Who are lesbian mothers? Findings from a large national sample. Paper presented at the 108th Annual Convention of the American Psychological Association, Washington, DC.
Bradford, J. B., & Ryan, C. (1988). *National lesbian health care survey: Final report.* National Lesbian and Gay Health Foundation, Washington, DC.
Brand, P. A., & Kidd, A. H. (1986). Frequency of physical aggression in heterosexual and female homosexual dyads. *Psychological Reports, 59*, 1307-1313.
Burke, L. K., & Follingstad, D. R. (1999). Violence in lesbian and gay relationships: Theory, prevalence, and correlational factors. *Clinical Psychology Review, 19*(5), 487-512.
Butke, M. (1995). Lesbians and sexual child abuse. In L.A. Fuentes (Ed.), *Sexual abuse in nine North American cultures*, pp. 236-258. Thousand Oaks, CA: Sage Publications.
Carlson, E. B., & Dalenberg, C. J. (2000). A conceptual framework for the impact of traumatic experiences. *Trauma, Violence, & Abuse, 1*(1), 4-28.

Crane, B., LaFrance, J., Leichtling, G., Nelson, B., & Silver, E. (1999). Lesbians and bisexual women working cooperatively to end domestic violence. In B. Leventhal & S. E. Lundy (Eds.), *Same-sex domestic violence: Strategies for change*, pp. 125-134. Thousand Oaks, CA: Sage Publications.

Descamps, M. J., Rothblum, E., Bradford, J., & Ryan, C (2000). Mental health impact of child sexual abuse, rape, intimate partner violence, and hate crimes in the National Lesbian Health Care Survey. *Journal of Gay & Lesbian Social Services, 11,* 27-55.

DiPlacido, J. (1998). Minority stress among lesbians, gay men, and bisexuals: A consequence of heterosexism, homophobia, and stigmatization. In G. M. Herek (Ed.), *Stigma and sexual orientation: Understanding prejudice against lesbians, gay men, and bisexuals*, pp. 138-159. Thousand Oaks, CA: Sage Publications.

Duncan, D. (1990). Prevalence of sexual assault victimization among heterosexual and gay/lesbian university students. *Psychological Reports, 59,* 1307-1313.

Gidycz, C. A., Coble, C. N., Latham, L., & Layman, M. J. (1993). Sexual assault experience in adulthood and prior victimization experiences: A prospective analysis. *Psychology of Women Quarterly, 17,* 151-168.

Greene, B. (1994). Lesbian women of color: Triple Jeopardy. In L. Comas-Diaz & B. Greene (Eds.), *Women of color: Integrating ethnic and gender identities in psychotherapy*, pp. 389-427. New York: Guilford.

Hall, J. (1998). Lesbians surviving childhood sexual abuse: Pivotal experiences related to sexual orientation, gender, and race. *Journal of Lesbian Studies, 2*(1), 7-28.

Harry, J. (1989). Parental physical abuse and sexual orientation in males. *Archives of Sexual Behavior, 18*(3), 251-261.

Herek, G. M., Gillis, J. R., Cogan, J. C., & Glunt, E. K. (1997). Hate crime victimization among lesbian, gay, and bisexual adults. *Journal of Interpersonal Violence, 12*(2), 195-215.

Hughes, T. L., Johnson, T., & Wilsnack, S. C. (2001). Sexual assault and alcohol abuse: A comparison of lesbians and heterosexual women. *Journal of Substance Abuse, 13,* 515-532.

Hughes, T. L., Haas, A. P., Razzano, L., Cassidy, R., & Matthews, A. (2000). Comparing lesbians' and heterosexual women's mental health: A multi-site survey. *Journal of Gay & Lesbian Social Services, 11*(1), 57-76.

Hunter, J. (1990). Violence against lesbian and gay male youths. *Journal of Interpersonal Violence, 5,* 295-300.

Koss, M. P., Goodman, L. A., Browne, A., Fitzgerald, L. F., Keita, G. P., & Russo, N. F. (1994). *No safe haven: Male violence against women at home, at work, and in the community.* Washington, DC: American Psychological Association.

Kruks, G. (1991). Gay and lesbian homeless/street youth: Special issues and concerns. *Journal of Adolescent Health, 12*(7), pp. 515-518.

Lock, J., & Steiner, H. (1999). Relationships between sexual orientation and coping styles of gay, lesbian, and bisexual adolescents from a community high school. *Journal of the Gay and Lesbian Medical Association, 3*(3), 77-82.

Messman-Moore, T. L., Long, P. J., & Siegfried, N. J. (2000). The revictimization of child sexual abuse survivors: An examination of the adjustment of college women with child sexual abuse, adult sexual assault, and adult physical abuse. *Child Maltreatment 5*(1), 18-27.

Moore, C. D., & Waterman, C. K. (1999). Predicting self-protection against sexual assault in dating relationships among heterosexual men and women, gay men, lesbians, and bisexuals. *Journal of College Student Development, 40*(2), 132-140.

Morris, J. F. (1997). *Set free: Lesbian mental health and the coming out process*. Unpublished doctoral dissertation, University of Vermont.

Morris, J. F., Waldo, C. R., & Rothblum, E. D. (2001). A model of predictors and outcomes of outness among lesbian and bisexual women. *American Journal of Orthopsychiatry, 71*(1), 61-71.

Neisen, J. H. (1993). Healing from cultural victimization: Recovery from shame due to heterosexism. *Journal of Gay & Lesbian Psychotherapy, 2*(1), 49-63.

Ochs, R. (1996). Biphobia: It goes more than two ways. In B. A. Firestein (Ed.), *Bisexuality: The psychology and politics of an invisible minority*. Thousand Oaks: Sage.

Otis, M. D., & Skinner, W. F. (1996). The prevalence of victimization and its effect on mental well-being among lesbian and gay people. *Journal of Homosexuality, 30*, 93-117.

Perry, S. M. (1995). Lesbian alcohol and marijuana use: Correlates of HIV risk behaviors and abusive relationships. *Journal of Psychoactive Drugs, 27*(4), 413-419.

Pilkington, N. W., & D'Augelli, A. R. (1995). Victimization of lesbian, gay, and bisexual youth in community settings. *Journal of Community Psychology, 23*, 33-56.

Roberts, S. J., & Sorensen, L. (1999). Prevalence of childhood sexual abuse and related sequelae in a lesbian population. *Journal of the Gay and Lesbian Medical Association, 3*(1), 11-19.

Root, M. P. (1996). Women of color and traumatic stress in "domestic captivity": Gender and race as disempowering statuses. In A. J. Marsella, M. J. Friedman, E. T. Gerrity, & R. M. Scurfield (Eds.), *Ethnocultural aspects of posttraumatic stress disorder: issues, research, and clinical applications*, pp. 363-387. Washington, DC: American Psychological Association.

Root, M. P. (1992). Reconstructing the impact of trauma on personality. In L. S. Brown & M. Ballou (Eds.), *Personality and psychopathology: Feminist reappraisals*, pp. 229-265. New York: Guilford.

Rothblum, E. D., & Factor, R. (2001). Lesbians and their sisters as a control group: Demographic and mental health factors. *Psychological Science, 12*(1), 63-69.

Russell, D. E. H., & Bolen, R. M. (2000). *The epidemic of rape and child sexual abuse in the United States*. Thousand Oaks, CA: Sage Publications.

Savin-Williams, R. C. (1994). Verbal and physical abuse as stressors in the lives of lesbian, gay male, and bisexual youth: Associations with school problems, running away, substance abuse, prostitution, and suicide. *Journal of Consulting and Clinical Psychology, 62*, 261-269.

Sulis, S. (1999). Battered bisexual women. In B. Leventhal & S. E. Lundy (Eds.), *Same-sex domestic violence: Strategies for change*, pp.173-180. Thousand Oaks, CA: Sage Publications.

Tjaden, P., Thoeness, N., & Allison, C. J. (1999). Comparing violence over the life span in samples of same-sex and opposite-sex cohabitants. *Violence and Victims, 14*(4), 413-425.

Walker, L. E. A. (1994). *Abused women and survivor therapy: A practical guide for the psychotherapist.* Washington, DC: American Psychological Association Press.

Weingourt, R. (1998). A comparison of heterosexual and homosexual long-term sexual relationships. *Archives of Psychiatric Nursing, 7*(2), 114-118.

Wyatt, G. E. (1992). The sociocultural context of African American and white American women's rape. *Journal of Social Issues, 48,* 77-91.

The Effects of Sexual Orientation on Body Image and Attitudes About Eating and Weight

Linda K. Owens
Tonda L. Hughes
Dawn Owens-Nicholson

Linda K. Owens, PhD, is affiliated with the University of Illinois at Urbana-Champaign.

Tonda L. Hughes, RN, PhD, FAAN, is affiliated with the University of Illinois at Chicago.

Dawn Owens-Nicholson, MA, is affiliated with the University of Illinois at Urbana-Champaign.

Address correspondence to: Linda K. Owens, 505 E. Green Street, Suite 3, Champaign, IL 61820 (E-mail: lindao@srl.uic.edu).

Merging of the data sets, data analysis, and preparation of this manuscript were supported by the Lesbian Health Fund of the Gay and Lesbian Medical Association, a Mental Health Services Research Grant on Women and Gender from the National Institute on Mental Health #1R24 MH54212, University of Illinois (UIC) Department of Psychiatry, and an Internal Research Support Grant (IRSP) from the UIC College of Nursing. The Chicago Board of Health and the Chicago Foundation for Women supported the Chicago survey. The New York survey was supported by a grant from the Professional Staff Congress of the City University of New York.

The authors would like to acknowledge the Lesbian Community Cancer Project and the following members of the research team who assisted with instrument development and data collection in the Chicago survey: Alice Dan, PhD, Ellie Emanuel, PhD (P.I. of the Minneapolis/St. Paul survey), Ann Pollinger Haas (P.I. of the New York City survey) Mary McCauly, BA, Carrol Smith, RN, MS, Sheila Healy, MSW, LCSW, Susan Guggenheim, BA, Jackie Anderson, PhD, Kathy Hull, MA, and Karen Williams, MS. In addition, the authors are grateful to Lisa Avery, PhD, Roberta Cassidy, MS, and Sonja Nelson, MSW, who assisted in merging the data sets and with data coding and analysis for the combined multi-site data, and to Tim Johnson who reviewed the manuscript.

[Haworth co-indexing entry note]: "The Effects of Sexual Orientation on Body Image and Attitudes About Eating and Weight." Owens, Linda K., Tonda L. Hughes, and Dawn Owens-Nicholson. Co-published simultaneously in *Journal of Lesbian Studies* (Harrington Park Press, an imprint of The Haworth Press, Inc.) Vol. 7, No. 1, 2003, pp. 15-33; and: *Mental Health Issues for Sexual Minority Women: Redefining Women's Mental Health* (ed: Tonda L. Hughes, Carrol Smith, and Alice Dan) Harrington Park Press, an imprint of The Haworth Press, Inc., 2003, pp. 15-33. Single or multiple copies of this article are available for a fee from The Haworth Document Delivery Service [1-800-HAWORTH, 9:00 a.m. - 5:00 p.m. (EST). E-mail address: getinfo@haworthpressinc.com].

SUMMARY. We assessed the effect of sexual orientation on body image and attitudes toward eating and weight using data collected from lesbians and heterosexual women in three US cities. Data were analyzed using ordinary least squares regression controlling for a number of demographic characteristics. Findings indicate that while lesbian sexual orientation is predictive of positive body image and fewer negative attitudes toward eating and weight, the effects are modest. Body mass index (BMI), frequency of exercise, race, and self-image were the strongest predictors of body image; BMI, race, and city of residence were the strongest predictors of attitudes toward eating and weight. The authors conclude that while belonging to a lesbian subculture may provide some protection against the societal imperative toward thinness, it likely does not counter the larger societal preference that women be thin.

KEYWORDS. Lesbians, sexual orientation, body image, eating disorders

Body image and eating disorders are primarily women's health issues. Women account for 90% of people diagnosed with eating disorders (Anderson, 1992). Research on the psychosocial correlates of eating disorders reveals that poor body image is one of the major contributors to dysfunctional attitudes about eating that are associated with anorexia and bulimia (Strong, Williamson, Netemeyer, & Geer, 2000; Taylor & Altman, 1997). Body image, in turn, is influenced by the degree to which women internalize social norms regarding femininity and beauty (Bergeron & Senn, 1998). Although norms regarding appearance affect all members of our society, they are applied much more strictly to women than to men (Bordo, 1993; Chrisler, 1991; Chrisler, 1994; Kuba & Hanchey, 1991). As a result, most women are dissatisfied with their bodies and perceive themselves as overweight, even when they are not (Fallon & Rozin, 1985; Rodin, Silberstein, & Striegel-Moore, 1985).

Aesthetic preferences for body shape and size vary from culture to culture and at different times in history. For example, research showing that African American culture places less emphasis on thinness and that women in that culture have better body image than white women (Cash & Henry, 1995; Parker, Nichter, Nichter, & Vuckovic, 1995; Rosen, Anthony, Booker, & Brown,

1991; Rucker & Cash, 1992) suggests that certain cultures may provide some insulation from contemporary society's strong preferences that women be thin.

The fact that men, in general, are more concerned with physical attractiveness in romantic/sexual partners than women is well established (Brand, Rothblum, & Solomon, 1992; Siever, 1994; Bergeron & Senn, 1998). In addition, norms regarding physical attractiveness have been constructed largely from a male perspective. Media images convey to women what they should look like if they want to be attractive to men. It follows, then, that women who are interested in men as romantic/sexual partners would give more credence to these images than women who are romantically/sexually attracted primarily to other women. As a consequence, lesbians may internalize society's messages about appearance to a lesser degree than heterosexual women (Bergeron & Senn, 1998; Rothblum, 1994). However, whether, or to what extent, lesbian culture buffers norms of the larger society regarding physical appearance is a subject of debate. Dworkin (1988) argues that lesbians are first and foremost women, and are therefore as susceptible as heterosexuals to internalizing societal norms regarding physical appearance.

Although a small amount of research on sexual orientation and body image has examined this question, the results have been contradictory. Bergeron and Senn (1998) found that women who internalize social norms regarding body image tend to have lower scores on body image scales, and that heterosexual women internalize these social norms to a much greater degree than do lesbians. Further, existing research suggests that compared with heterosexual women, lesbians place less emphasis on physical attractiveness (Siever, 1994; Gettelman & Thompson, 1993), have bigger ideal body sizes (Herzog, Newman, Yeh, & Warshaw, 1992), and are less likely to have negative body images or to view themselves as overweight (French, Story, Remafedi, Resnick, & Blum, 1996). However, Siever (1994) and Beren, Hayden, Wilfley, and Grilo (1996) found no differences between lesbians and heterosexual women in terms of body dissatisfaction.

Another reason that lesbians are thought to be protected from negative norms regarding body size is the assumption that a higher proportion of lesbians are feminists. Feminist ideals include more tolerance of diversity in body size (Rothblum, 1994). However, research assessing the effects of feminist orientation has also produced conflicting results. For example, while Ojerholm and Rothblum (1999) found that a feminist identity was associated with more tolerance toward body size in others, it was not statistically related to respondents' own body image. Bergeron and Senn (1998) found that feminists scored lower on four scales measuring body dissatisfaction and higher on one scale measuring body satisfaction, but lesbians were no more likely than heterosexual women to identify as feminist.

One explanation for the lack of consistent findings regarding the relationship between internalization of social norms and body image is that lesbians' scores on body image scales may reflect politically correct, rather than personal, attitudes (Siever, 1994; Bergeron & Senn, 1998). In other words, lesbians may be aware of the damaging effects of social norms about body size and may think that they shouldn't buy into them–but may do so anyway. Ojerholm and Rothblum's (1999) finding that feminism was associated with more positive attitudes about other's weight but not respondents' own weight supports this hypothesis.

Whether or how the relationship between body image and eating disorders differs for lesbians and heterosexual women is also unclear. Some studies suggest that lesbians report fewer attitudes associated with eating disorders (Siever, 1994; Gettelman & Thompson, 1993; Herzog et al., 1992), while others find that they diet and binge to the same degree as heterosexual women (French et al., 1996).

In summary, prior research in this area has hypothesized that lesbians have better body image and fewer attitudes associated with disordered eating than heterosexual women for two main reasons. First, lesbians typically partner with other women and women place less emphasis on partners' physical attractiveness than do men. Second, lesbians are believed to be more likely than heterosexual women to hold feminist attitudes that include acceptance of a wider range of body sizes. However, because findings regarding these hypotheses have been inconsistent, and sometimes contradictory, additional research is warranted. Thus, given the compelling logic underlying the hypotheses in previous research, we predicted that lesbians would have more positive body image and show fewer attitudes associated with disordered eating. Beregon and Senn's (1998) argument that sexual orientation serves to attenuate rather than negate the internalization of social norms underlies the hypotheses of this study.

METHODS

This study was designed to address several of the common methodological weaknesses that characterize research on lesbian health, such as small homogeneous samples, lack of heterosexual comparison groups, and inconsistent or absent definitions of sexual orientation (Solarz, 1999). The study was initiated by the Chicago Lesbian Community Cancer Project (LCCP) to collect data on general health status and the behavioral and environmental health risks of lesbians in Chicago. A survey instrument was developed between January 1993 and February 1994 by an interdisciplinary team of women from various universities and community groups, including volunteers of LCCP. The questionnaire was reviewed in focus groups and piloted in Chicago in 1994-1995. Subsequently, the questionnaire was slightly revised and data were collected in Minneapolis/St. Paul and in New York City. Questions related to sexual orientation and relationship status are the only ones used in these analyses that were revised between the Chicago survey and later surveys in New York and Minneapolis/St. Paul. Variables derived from these questions are described in detail later in the paper.

Sampling and Data Collection

Because lesbians are a relatively small subgroup of the general population (Laumann, Gagnon, Michael, & Michaels, 1994), many studies focusing on body image have relied on convenience samples located in or around universities (Siever, 1994; Gettelman & Thompson, 1993; Herzog et al., 1992; Beren et al., 1996; Strong et al., 2000). In addition, while many of the heterosexual samples were recruited through universities, lesbians were more often recruited from gay and lesbian organizations in the communities surrounding the universities. Other differences in demographic characteristics of the samples, such as age and geography, included in these studies may also account for some of the inconsistencies in study findings (French et al., 1996; Siever, 1994).

To obtain as diverse a sample as possible, a broad range of recruitment methods and sources were used in the current study. In addition to distributing the survey instrument in numerous formal and informal lesbian settings (e.g., potluck dinners; discussion groups; bookstores; softball and bowling leagues; coffee houses; college, social, support, therapeutic, musical, and political groups and organizations), participants were sought through informal networks of friends and coworkers.

Comparison groups of heterosexual women were obtained by asking lesbians who completed the survey to give a second copy (a color-coded duplicate of the original) to a female friend, acquaintance, or colleague with a job (or in the case of students, homemakers, or retirees, a role) as similar as possible to the lesbians' own. Because we anticipated that this method would result in an adequately large sample of heterosexual women with background characteristics similar to those of the lesbian group, we did not specify in the Chicago survey that the work-role counterpart should be heterosexual. Given the less than optimal results (a sample consisting of only about half as many heterosexual women as lesbians), instructions provided in the Minnesota (MN) and New

York (NY) surveys specified that the work-role counterpart be a woman *whom the lesbian knew or presumed to be heterosexual.* In addition, unlike in the other two sites, in NY lesbian respondents were given a small incentive of $15.00 for completing the survey and for recruiting a work-role counterpart into the study; work-role counterparts were given $10.00 for completing the survey. Further representatives of harder-to-reach lesbian groups who agreed to act as distributors of the survey were paid $5.00 for each completed survey they returned. These strategies resulted in a more racially diverse sample and a larger proportion of heterosexual respondents in NY than in the other two survey sites.

In all three sites data were collected from lesbians in groups (e.g., organized gatherings at bookstores) or survey instruments were distributed to individuals. Lesbians and work-role counterparts were given instructions to complete and return the survey in person (in a sealed return envelope) or by mail in a postage-paid, pre-addressed envelope. No code numbers or other identifiers were included so respondents could be confident that their responses were anonymous. In each of the sites, approximately one-half of the distributed surveys were returned; thus, we estimated the overall response rate to be approximately 48%, with no appreciable difference by site.

Instrument and Measures

The survey instrument covered a broad range of areas that impact women's health. These included personal health history (e.g., general, menstrual, and gynecological health), health-related practices (e.g., diet, health screening, alternative health practices), mental health (including physical and sexual abuse, use of legal and illegal substances, depression, and suicide ideation and attempts), access to and use of health services, relationships and supports, and background demographic information. Almost all questionnaire items were closed-ended.

Sexual Orientation. Because questions assessing self-identity were included only in the Chicago survey, the definition of sexual orientation used in the analyses presented here is based on responses to two survey questions: (1) current sexual interest or attraction, and (2) sexual behavior in the year before completing the survey. Both questions include the following response categories: "only men," "mostly men," "equally men and women," "mostly women," and "only women." The question concerning sexual behavior also included the category, "I have not had sex in the past year." By summarizing the combinations of responses to these two questions, we created two primary categories of sexual orientation–which we labeled lesbian and heterosexual. For example, women who reported that they were only or mostly attracted to women and who were sexually active only with women (or not sexually active with either women or men) in the past year were classified as lesbian. Similarly, women who were only or mostly attracted to men and who were sexually active only with men (or neither men or women) were considered to be heterosexual for purposes of these analyses. Women who were bisexual or whose responses were inconsistent on the behavior and attraction questions (less than 5% of the samples) were omitted from the analyses.

Demographic Variables. We coded race as a dichotomous indicator of whether or not the respondent was African American. Hispanic respondents were assigned a value of 1 for ethnicity; all other respondents were assigned a value of 0. Respondent's age (in years) was measured continuously. The question about annual household income asked respondents to choose one of eight income range categories. We recoded these to the midpoint of the interval and report the median income for lesbian and heterosexual women. The original question about level of education asked respondents to choose from four categories (i.e., high school or less, some college, bachelor's degree, professional or advanced degree). We computed a proxy variable indicating the approximate number of years of formal education (range = 10 to 22 years).

Finally, the question about relationship status in Chicago asked respondents if they were legally married. If not married, they were then asked if they were in a committed relationship. In New York and Minneapolis/St. Paul women were asked to select from the following categories the one that best described their current relationship status: single, not dating; single, dating casually; single, dating someone seriously/engaged; in a committed relationship but not legally married; legally married; and other. As in the Chicago sample, the definition of "committed relationship" was left to the interpretation of the respondents. We constructed a dummy variable to indicate whether or not the respondent was in a committed relationship. In the Chicago sample, women who reported that they were legally married or in a committed relationship were given a value of 1 on this variable. In the New York and Minneapolis/St. Paul samples, women who were dating someone seriously or engaged, in a committed relationship, or legally married were given a value of 1.

Site. Data were collected in Chicago, Minneapolis/St. Paul, and New York City. To control for differences in data collection methods as well as to test for differences in geographic residence, two dichotomous variables were included in the analyses–one indicating the respondent was from New York and the other indicating the respondent was from Chicago. Coefficients on these two variables show the effect of living in that location compared to living in Minneapolis/St. Paul.

Body Mass Index (BMI). Respondents were asked to provide their height and weight in ranges. For example, one height category was 5'0" to 5'3", and one weight category was 121 to 135 pounds. We calculated body mass index (BMI) using the standard formula: BMI = weight in kilograms divided by height in meters squared. Because height and weight were available only in ranges, we used the midpoint of the height and weight range intervals. Using the example above, we calculated BMI using a height of 5 feet 1 1/2 inches and a weight of 128 pounds, resulting in a BMI of approximately 23.8. To determine whether using the upper or lower height and weight ranges differed substantially from analyses using the midpoints we ran the analyses using these values. Results for the three sets of analyses differed only minimally.

Frequency of Exercise. Respondents were asked how often they exercise. Answers range from never (0) to daily (4).

Self-Image Index. This index was created from eight semantic differential questions (e.g., "I am very self-confident/not at all self-confident," "I am very much in control of my life/not at all in control of my life"). Respondents rated themselves along a 5-point continuum between the two opposite positions. Scores ranged from 0 to 4. A higher value on the index indicates poorer self-image. The Cronbach alpha reliability coefficient for this index is .85.

Body Image Index. As Thompson et al. (1990) point out, body image is a broad construct that can encompass a number ways of relating to one's body. As a consequence, there are many ways body image has been measured (e.g., Ben-Tovim & Walker, 1991; Cooper, Taylor, Cooper, & Fairburn, 1987). For these analyses we used six indicators of how women feel about their bodies to construct a body image index. The index items were scored on a 4-point Likert-type scale and represent respondents' level of agreement with the following statements: (1) Most of the time I am happy with the way I look; (2) I am not satisfied with my weight; (3) I wish that I were in better physical condition; (4) I am proud of my body; (5) I often feel ugly and unattractive; and (6) I feel strong and healthy. Responses ranged from strongly agree (4) to strongly disagree (0). Where appropriate, items were recoded so all six items share the same valence. The index is the mean value of the six items, where a higher value indicates a more positive body image. Cronbach's alpha reliability coefficient for this index is .83.

Attitudes Toward Eating and Weight Index. We created an index of attitudes toward eating and weight. This index consists of five items scored on a 5-point scale, with 0 (never) to always (4) indicating the respondents' level of agreement with the following statements: (1) I am terrified about being overweight; (2) I think about burning calories when I exercise; (3) Eating too much makes me feel gross and ugly; (4) When I am upset, I worry that I will start eating; and (5) I think about dieting. Scores were summed to calculate an index score, where a higher value indicates attitudes toward eating and weight that are more consistent with disordered eating. Cronbach's alpha for this index was .84.

DATA ANALYSES

Frequency distributions and measures of central tendency and dispersion summarize the demographic characteristics of the sample. T-tests were used to test for differences between lesbian and heterosexual women on continuous variables. Ordinary least squares regression analyses were conducted to explore the relative contributions of several variables in predicting body image and attitudes toward eating and weight. All significant differences reported here have probabilities of p ≤ .05. Using ordinary least squares regression, we estimated two separate models, one in which body image was the dependent variable and the other in which attitudes toward eating and weight were the dependent variable.

Three of the control variables in this analysis merit particular mention–age, race, and study site. At younger ages the influence of society at large on a woman's identity may be greater than the influence of lesbian subculture (Franzoi & Shields, 1984). In addition, younger women may be less likely to have developed a positive lesbian identity (Garnets & Kimmel, 1993). Therefore, we control for age to address potential developmental differences in vulnerability to social messages. Race is of particular importance as well, as research has shown that African American women have better body image than white women (Cash & Henry, 1995; Parker, Nichter, Nichter, & Vuckovic, 1995; Rosen, Anthony, Booker, & Brown, 1991; Rucker & Cash, 1992). Finally, the inclusion of study site as a control variable is important for several reasons (see Table 1). First, the data collection methods differed somewhat between the sites. Second, the demographic characteristics of respondents varied between sites. Third, most studies on this topic collected data from one location, typically near a university. Including site in the analyses may provide information about the degree to which geography influences body image. If race and sexual orientation can be considered subcultures that exert their own impact on body image, it is not unreasonable to assume that the city where one resides may also influence body image.

TABLE 1. Data Collection Sites, Dates, and Sample Sizes

Data Collection Sites	Dates	Lesbians	Heterosexual Women	Total
Chicago	94-95	273	134	407
Minneapolis/St. Paul	94-95	160	67	227
New York	95-96	117	78	195
Total		550	279	829

Initial estimations included all independent variables. We arrived at the final models through the iterative deletion of insignificant variables. All variables remaining in the models are significant at the .05 level.

RESULTS

Description of the Sample

Respondents who had missing data on any of the study variables were excluded. Thus, 776 women (518 lesbian and 258 heterosexual) are included in the body image analysis, and 786 women (525 lesbian and 261 heterosexual) are included in the attitudes toward eating and weight analysis.

As mentioned above, there were several important differences in the sample based on study site (see Table 2). For example, lesbians from NY were older than those from Chicago and MN. Race of the samples also differed by site. The sample from MN was the most racially homogeneous: 87% of lesbians and 92% of the heterosexual women were European American. In the Chicago sample, 82% of the lesbians and 75% of the heterosexual women were European American. Conversely, in the NY sample, only 50% of lesbians and 44% of heterosexual women were European American. Women in Chicago reported the highest levels of education and women in NY the lowest (p < .001). European American lesbians were less likely than African American lesbians to have a high school education or less (9% compared with 35%), and more

TABLE 2. Selected Demographic Characteristics by Site

Demographic Characteristic	Site					
	Chicago		Minneapolis/St. Paul		New York City	
	Lesbian	Heterosexual	Lesbian	Heterosexual	Lesbian	Heterosexual
N	273	134	160	67	117	78
Mean Age	42.4	44.0	41.9	39.7	45.8	41.9
African-American	23 (8.4%)	14 (10.4%)	6 (3.8%)	2 (3.0%)	46 (39.3%)	26 (33.3%)
Hispanic	7 (2.6%)	9 (6.7%)	1 (.6%)	2 (3.0%)	12 (10.3%)	10 (12.8%)
Mean Years Education	16.2	16.2	16.1	15.9	15.6	15.3
Mean Family Income	$25,767	$29,008	$22,613	$27,761	$32,293	$35,078
In a Committed Relationship	158 (57.9%)	85 (63.4%)	107 (66.9%)	41 (61.2%)	78 (66.7%)	50 (64.1%)

likely to have advanced degrees (43% compared with 20%) (p < .001). The same pattern of results was found between European American and African American heterosexual women (p < .001). Thus, the difference in education levels between New York and the other two sites can likely be attributed to race differences among the three sites. Given differences in study sites found in the bivariate analyses, the regression analyses reported below control for site and demographic differences.

Ages of the women in this study ranged from 20 to 86 years old (the overall mean age of the sample is 42.6 years). The mean ages of the lesbian and heterosexual respondents were similar: t (806) = 1.305, p = .192.

The sample was more racially diverse than many included in lesbian health studies. Nevertheless, the majority of the participants were European American (78% of lesbians and 74% of heterosexual women); only 11% of the lesbians and 14% of the heterosexual women were African American. The remainder of the sample (11% lesbian and 12% heterosexual) was Hispanic, Asian American, Native American, or of another racial/ethnic background.

Similar to most other studies of lesbians, this sample was well-educated overall. Almost one-half (48% of both groups) had completed some college and more than one-third (38% lesbians and 36% heterosexuals) had an advanced degree. Relatively few of the lesbians (14%) or heterosexual women (16%) reported that they had a high school education or less.

The modal category for household income for both the lesbian and heterosexual women was $21,000-$35,999.

Exactly the same proportions of lesbians and heterosexual women (52%) reported that they currently live with a partner or spouse. Two-thirds (66%) of the lesbians reported that they are in a committed relationship. This proportion is similar to that reported by the heterosexual women when combining those who reported being legally married (53%) and those in a committed relationship (18%). Interestingly, 11% of lesbians reported that they were currently legally married. A substantial portion of these lesbians also responded that they were "in a committed relationship, not legally married." This may indicate that some lesbians consider themselves married to their female partners, even though these relationships cannot be legally sanctioned. There were no statistically significant differences between lesbians and heterosexual women on any of the key demographic variables.

Bivariate Relationships

Body Mass Index. Lesbians in this study had a slightly higher BMI than did heterosexual women (29.6 vs. 28.2, t(688) = 3.003, p = .003). The average BMI for both groups of women exceeds the recommendation of 27.3/kg/m^2 by the office of the surgeon general (DHHS, 1988). In addition, 36.8% of lesbians were above the recommended BMI compared to 30.1% of heterosexual women. Although we could not calculate exact BMI, there is no reason to suspect that lesbians would be any farther or closer to the midpoint of the ranges used than heterosexual women. Therefore, it is unlikely that the error in the BMI calculation is biased more for one group than the other.

Body Image and Attitudes About Eating and Weight. Lesbians had somewhat higher scores on the body image index and lower scores on the index measuring attitudes toward eating and weight that are associated with disordered eating. However, the differences were not significant (2.45 vs. 2.39, $t(826) = 1.861$, $p = .063$ for body image; 1.65 vs. 1.78 , $t(826) = -1.91$, $p = .056$ for attitudes toward eating and weight.

After running bivariate comparisons between lesbians and heterosexual women, predictors of body image and attitudes toward eating and weight were examined using regression analyses.

Multivariate Analyses

Body Image

Results of the regression analysis examining predictors of body image are summarized in Table 3. Although smaller than most other effects, sexual orientation was predictive of body image, indicating that lesbians had higher

TABLE 3. Results of Regression of Body Image on Independent Variables

	Unstandardized Coefficients		Standardized Coefficients	t-value	Sig.
	B	Std. Error	Beta		
Constant	3.252	.106		30.818	.000
African American	.170	.047	.127	3.639	.000
Frequency of Exercise	.059	.015	.132	4.011	.000
Household Income	−.000002	.000	−.065	−1.971	.049
Lesbian	.096	.031	.099	3.078	.002
Mean BMI	−.029	.002	−.425	−12.999	.000
Self-Image	−.091	.023	−.125	−3.918	.000
Chicago	−.097	.035	−.106	−2.797	.005
New York	−.090	.045	−.083	−2.024	.043

$R^2 = .24$

(more positive) scores on the body image index. However, the low Beta value (.099) indicates that this relationship is moderate at best.

In this study BMI was the strongest predictor of body image. Women with higher BMIs had poorer body image. Not surprisingly, greater frequency of exercise was also predictive of more positive body image (Beta = .132). Following exercise, race and self-image had the next largest effects (Beta = .127 and −.125 respectively). African American women and those with lower self-image scores also tended to score more positively on the body image index.

Interestingly, body image also differed by study site. Women from both New York and Chicago scored lower on the body image index than did women from Minneapolis/St. Paul (Beta = −.083 and −.106 respectively). Finally, household income had a small, negative effect on body image, with higher income associated with a lower score (Beta = −.065). Together, these variables accounted for 24% of the variance in body image.

Attitudes Toward Eating and Weight

We next examined predictors of attitudes toward eating and weight. As reflected in Table 4, lesbian sexual orientation had a small negative effect on this variable (Beta = −.083) indicating that lesbians are less likely than heterosexual women to have attitudes associated with disordered eating.

Like body image, the strongest predictor of attitudes toward eating and weight was higher BMI score (Beta = .288). Following BMI, study site was the strongest predictor, with respondents in both New York and Chicago more

TABLE 4. Results of Regression of Attitudes About Eating and Weight on Independent Variables

	Unstandardized Coefficients		Standardized Coefficients	t	Sig.
	B	Std. Error	Beta		
Constant	.893	.187		4.777	.000
African American	−.313	.100	−.114	−3.115	.002
Lesbian	−.166	.069	−.083	−2.417	.016
Mean BMI	.041	.005	.288	8.321	.000
Chicago	.263	.076	.139	3.438	.001
New York	.464	.097	.206	4.785	.000
Age	−.009	.003	−.101	−2.966	.003

$R^2 = .11$

likely to report attitudes associated with disordered eating than respondents from Minneapolis/St. Paul (Beta = .207 and .139 respectively). Again, race appeared to have a protective effect, with African Americans having fewer attitudes associated with disordered eating than women of other races (Beta = −.114). Although insignificant in the body image model, age was a significant predictor of tendency toward disordered eating. Older women had fewer attitudes associated with disordered eating than younger women (Beta = −.101). Given that these variables account for only 11% of the variance in the model it is clear that other unmeasured factors account for the majority of variance in attitudes toward eating and weight.

Few of the demographic factors were significant predictors of body image or attitudes toward eating and weight. For example, committed relationship status, Hispanic ethnicity, and years of education predicted neither body image nor attitudes toward eating and weight. Age was not a significant predictor of body image. Self-image, frequency of exercise, and household income were not predictive of attitudes toward eating and weight.

DISCUSSION

The hypothesis that lesbians would score higher on body image and have fewer attitudes associated with disordered eating was supported by findings from this study. Further, like findings from other recent studies (e.g., Markovic, Aaron, Danielson, Schmidt, & Janosky, 1999; Valanis et al., 2000), lesbians were more likely than heterosexual women to be obese based on the recommended BMI of 27.3 kg/m^2 (DHHS, 1988).

Given research findings suggesting that lesbian subculture may buffer the larger culture's emphasis on thinness and other aspects of appearance, we expected lesbians to have a better body image and fewer attitudes associated with disordered eating than heterosexual women. However, we agree with Dworkin (1988) that one would not expect the effects of a subculture joined by women later in life (and to varying degrees) to have a stronger impact than the larger culture to which women belong. In other words, although the lesbian subculture may offer some protection, it probably does not negate the effects of society at large. This may explain why the effects of lesbian sexual orientation on body image and attitudes toward eating and weight were relatively small.

The lesbian community/subculture is only one subculture in which lesbians live. Other subcultures may have independent effects on a lesbian's (or heterosexual woman's) attitudes toward her body or eating. For example, consistent with earlier research, African American women in our study also had higher scores on the body image index and fewer attitudes associated with disordered eating. In addition, our findings suggest that cultural influences predominant in various demographic locations may also have an impact on these attitudes. Women living in Minneapolis had higher scores on the body image index and fewer attitudes associated with disordered eating. Although we know of no data to support this, it is possible that because New York City and Chicago are focal points in the fashion industry, women who live in these cities may be more fashion and body conscious. Taken together, the effects of sexual orientation, race, and location of residence suggest that the various subcultures to which women belong may each influence the way they relate to their bodies and to food—sexual orientation appears to be only one influence.

Research has shown that body image is highly correlated with self-esteem (Franzoi & Shields, 1984; Lerner & Karabenick, 1974). Therefore, the prevalence of women's dissatisfaction with their bodies (Fallon & Rozin, 1985) points to a potentially serious mental health problem. This research and the studies cited here suggest that even though lesbians may be protected to some degree from cultural messages of ideal beauty—and the damage such messages can do—no woman is immune.

While lesbians may be somewhat protected from cultural messages regarding appearance, it is likely that other mental health consequences result from belonging to a stigmatized minority group. For example, although we did not examine binge eating in this study, it is possible that lesbians may be at risk for binge eating in response to stress associated with their sexual orientation (Heffernan, 1996). In separate analyses of data from the multi-site study, greater number of stigmatized statuses was associated with current and lifetime smoking, and smoking in response to stress (Hughes, Johnson, & Matthews, under review).

The fact that BMI had the strongest impact on body image and attitudes toward eating and weight shows that larger women have greater problems with body image. Because of the potential health consequences of higher BMIs (e.g., diabetes, cardiovascular disease) the importance of obesity cannot be disregarded. However, the cultural imperative toward thinness is about appearance, not health, and only serves to add emotional distress to existing weight-related physical problems.

Interventions are needed that address the overall health of women, for the sake of their own well-being, rather than for a cultural ideal. Such interventions should emphasize both sound nutrition and regular exercise as well as building a healthy sense of self that is less vulnerable to societal messages and gender-role norms.

Limitations

These findings must be interpreted in light of the limitations of the data. First, although the lesbian sample was large and was drawn from several areas of the United States, it cannot be assumed to represent the population of women who identify as lesbian. As with other volunteer-based studies, there may be a tendency for bias toward including more or less healthy participants and thus under or overestimating the prevalence of health risks such as obesity, poor body image, or attitudes associated with disordered eating. However, the method we used to obtain the heterosexual group provides a comparison that controls for many demographic and life-experience factors–other than sexual orientation–that might have influenced the variables in the study. Therefore, differences found between these two groups can more confidently be attributed to sexual orientation (Hughes, Wilsnack, & Johnson, in press). In addition, the fact that the questionnaire was revised slightly following data collection in Chicago also presented some difficulties with standardization of variables (e.g., defining "committed relationship").

A second limitation of this study is our operational definition of sexual orientation. We categorized women as lesbian or heterosexual on the basis of their responses to questions about same-sex behavior and attraction. Although sexual identity is generally highly correlated with behavior and attraction (Hughes, Haas, & Avery, 1997; Laumann, Gagnon, Michael, & Michaels, 1994), a substantial proportion of women who have sex with other women do not identify as lesbian. Thus, different definitions of sexual orientation may be associated with different levels of body image and different patterns of eating and weight.

Third, because the data analyzed in this study were collected for a general health needs assessment and not with a specific interest in body image or eating disorders, the measures used have clear limitations. The validity of the two scales used in these analyses is untested. Further research using standardized measures are needed to more clearly assess differences between lesbians and heterosexual women.

Fourth, the questionnaire did not include questions measuring current depression. Only a question about treatment for depression at some time in the past was included. Other research has identified current depression as a potential risk factor for eating disorders (Striegel-Moore, Silberstein, & Rodin, 1986; Veron-Guidry, Williamson, & Netemeyer, 1997. It is possible that the amount of variance explained by our model would have been greater if we included a measure of current depression.

Finally, although reporting height and weight in ranges may be less threatening to respondents and therefore lead to less item nonresponse, it presents a potentially serious measurement problem. For many respondents, we can not precisely identify whether or not their BMI falls into the surgeon general's definition of overweight (BMI of 25 or higher). In fact, we were able to definitively determine whether respondents were overweight according to the surgeon general's definition in 63% of the cases. This problem can be easily addressed in future studies by asking for specific height and weight values.

Despite these limitations, this study is one of few that have examined body image and attitudes associated with disordered eating in an older sample of lesbians, and one of even fewer studies that include a comparison group of heterosexual women. We suggest that studies with larger groups of racial/ethnic minority lesbians and those with lower levels of education be conducted to more systematically examine the influence of sexual orientation on body image. In addition, studies are needed that examine lesbians' eating and dieting patterns, and motivations for binge eating in greater depth.

CONCLUSION

While lesbian sexual orientation may buffer societal pressure to be thin and contribute to more positive body image, lesbians may be at overall greater health risk because of higher BMI. Greater knowledge of how lesbian and heterosexual women differ can inform and guide prevention and treatment programs aimed at reducing eating disorders and increasing overall mental health.

REFERENCES

Anderson, A.E. (1992). Males with eating disorders. In J. Yager, H.E. Gwirtsman, & C.K. Edelstein (Eds.), *Special problems in managing eating disorders* (pp. 87-118). Washington, DC: American Psychiatric Press.
Ben-Tovim, D.I., & Walker, M.K. (1991). The development of the Ben-Tovim-Walker Body Attitudes Questionnaire (BAQ), a new measure of women's attitudes towards their own bodies. *Psychological Medicine, 21,* 775-84.
Beren, S.E., Hayden, H.A., Wilfley, D.E., & Grilo, C.M. (1996). The influence of sexual orientation on body dissatisfaction in adult men and women. *International Journal of Eating Disorders, 20*(2), 135-141.
Bergeron, S.M., & Senn, C.Y. (1998). Body image and sociocultural norms. *Psychology of Women Quarterly, 22,* 385-401.
Bordo, S. (1993). *Unbearable weight. Feminism, Western culture and the body.* Berkeley: University of California Press.
Brand, P.A., Rothblum, E.D., & Solomon, L.J. (1992). A comparison of lesbians, gay men, and heterosexuals on weight and restrained eating. *International Journal of Eating Disorders, 11,* 253-259.

Cash, T.F., & Henry, P.E. (1995). Women's body images: The result of a national survey in the U.S.A. *Sex Roles, 33,* 19-28.

Chrisler, J.C. (1991). Out of control and eating disordered. In N. Van Den Bergh (Ed.), *Feminist perspectives on addictions* (pp. 139-149). New York: Springer Publishing Company.

Chrisler, J.C. (1994). Reframing women's weight: Does thin equal healthy? In A.J. Dan (Ed.), *Reframing women's health: Multidisciplinary research and practice* (pp. 330-338). Thousand Oaks, CA: Sage.

Cooper, P.J., Taylor, M.J., Cooper, Z., & Fairburn, C.G. (1987). The development and validation of the Body Shape Questionnaire. *International Journal of Eating Disorders, 6,* 485-494.

Department of Health and Human Services (DHHS) (1988). *Surgeon General's report on nutrition and health.* DHHS Pub. 88-50210: Washington, DC.

Dworkin, S.H. (1988). Not in a man's image: Lesbians and the cultural oppression of body image. *Women & Therapy, 8,* 27-39.

Fallon, A.E., & Rozin, P. (1985). Sex difference in perceptions of desirable body shape. *Journal of Abnormal Psychology, 94,* 102-105.

Franzoi, S.E., & Shields, S.A. (1984). The Body Esteem Scale: Multidimensional structure and sex differences in a college population. *Journal of Personality Assessment, 48,* 173-178.

French, S.A., Story, M., Remafedi, G., Resnick, M.D., & Blum, R.W. (1996). Sexual orientation and prevalence of body dissatisfaction and eating disordered behaviors: A population-based study of adolescents. *International Journal of Eating Disorders, 19*(2), 119-126.

Garnets, L.A., & Kimmel, D.C. (Eds) (1993). *Psychological perspectives on lesbian and gay male experiences.* New York: Columbia University Press.

Gettelman, T.E., & Thompson, J.K. (1993). Actual differences and stereotypical perceptions in body image and eating disturbances: A comparison of male and female heterosexual and homosexual samples. *Sex Roles, 29*(7/8), 545-562.

Heffernan, K. (1996). Eating disorders and weight concern among lesbians. *International Journal of Eating Disorders, 19*(2), 127-138.

Herzog, D.B., Newman, K.L., Yeh, C.J., & Warshaw, M. (1992). Body image satisfaction in homosexual and heterosexual women. *International Journal of Eating Disorders, 11*(4), 391-396.

Hughes, T.L., Johnson, T., & Matthews, A. (under review). Comparison of rates of smoking and smoking in response to stress in a multi-site study of lesbians and heterosexual women.

Hughes, T.L., Haas, A.P., & Avery, L. (1997). Lesbians and mental health: Preliminary results from the Chicago Women's Health Survey. *Journal of the Gay and Lesbian Medical Association,1,* 133-144.

Hughes, T.L., Wilsnack, S.C., & Johnson, T. (in press). Lesbians' mental health and alcohol use: Research challenges and findings. In A. Omoto & H. Kurtzman (Eds.), *Recent research on sexual orientation, mental health, and substance abuse.* Washington, DC: APA Books.

Kuba, S.A., & Hanchey, S.G. (1991). Reclaiming women's bodies: A feminist perspective on eating disorders. In N. Van Den Bergh (Ed.), *Feminist perspectives on addictions* (pp. 125-137). New York: Springer Publishing Company.

Laumann, E.O., Gagnon, J.H., Michael, R.T., & Michaels, S. (1994). *The social organization of sexuality: Sexual practices in the United States.* Chicago, IL: University of Chicago Press.

Lerner, R.M., & Karabenick, S.A. (1974). Physical attractiveness, body attitudes, and self-concept in late adolescents. *Journal of Youth and Adolescence, 3,* 307-316.

Markovic, N., Aaron, D.J., Danielson, M.E., Schmidt, N.J., & Janosky, J.E. (1999). Lesbians and cardiovascular diseases (CVD) risk factors. *American Journal of Epidemiology, 149*(11), Supplement, p S60.

Ojerholm, A.J., & Rothblum, E.D. (1999). The relationships of body image, feminism and sexual orientation in college women. *Feminism & Psychology, 9*(4), 431-448.

Parker, S., Nichter, M., Nichter, M., & Vuckovic, N. (1995). Body image and weight concerns among African-American and White adolescent females: Differences that make a difference. *Human Organization, 54*(2), 103-114.

Rodin, J., Silberstein, L.R., & Striegel-Moore, R.H. (1985). Women and weight: A normative discontent. In T.B. Sonderegger (Ed.), *Nebraska symposium on motivation; Vol. 32. Psychology and gender* (pp. 267-307). Lincoln: University of Nebraska Press.

Rosen, E.F., Anthony, D.L., Booker, K.M., & Brown, T.L. (1991). A comparison of eating disorder scores among African-American and White college females. *Bulletin of the Psychonomic Society, 29*(1), 65-66.

Rothblum, E.D. (1994). Lesbians and physical appearance: Which model applies? In B. Green and G.M. Herek (Eds.), *Lesbian and gay psychology: Theory, research, and clinical applications.* Thousand Oaks: Sage Publications.

Rucker, C.E., & Cash, T.F. (1992). Body images, body-size perceptions, and eating behaviors among African-American and White college women. *International Journal of Eating Disorders, 12*(3), 291-299.

Siever, M.D. (1994). Sexual orientation and gender as factors in socioculturally acquired vulnerability to body dissatisfaction and eating disorders. *Journal of Consulting and Clinical Psychology, 62*(2), 252-260.

Solarz, A.L. (1999). *Lesbian health. Current assessment and directions for the future.* National Academy Press: Institute of Medicine.

Striegel-Moore, R.H., Silberstein, L.R., & Rodin, J. (1986). Toward an understanding of risk factors for bulimia. *American Psychologist, 41,* 246-263.

Strong, S.M., Williamson, D.A., Netemeyer, R.G., & Geer, J.H. (2000). Eating disorder symptoms and concerns about body differ as a function of gender and sexual orientation. *Journal of Social and Clinical Psychology, 19*(2), 240-255.

Taylor, C.B., & Altman, T. (1997). Priorities in prevention research for eating disorders. *Psychopharmacology Bulletin, 33,* 413-417.

Valanis, B.G., Bowen, D.J., Bassford, T., Whitlock, E., Charney, P., & Carter, R.A. (2000). Sexual orientation and health: Comparisons in the Women's Health Initiative Sample. *Archives of Family Medicine, 9*(9), 843-853.

Veron-Guidry, S.P., Williamson, D.A., & Netemeyer, R.G. (1997). Structural modeling analysis of risk factors for eating disorders in children and preadolescents. *Eating Disorders: Journal of Treatment and Prevention, 5,* 15-27.

No Reflection in the Mirror: Challenges for Disabled Lesbians Accessing Mental Health Services

Corbett J. O'Toole

Allison A. Brown

SUMMARY. Lesbians with disabilities have atypical life experiences–they are virtually invisible within the mainstream culture. Both women with disabilities and lesbians experience societal, familial and economic pressures that directly impact their lives and the range of options available to them. When a lesbian is also a woman with a disability, the combination of these pressures has important mental health implications. This article explores the issues and barriers related to disabled lesbians accessing mental health services. Because no systematic research on the mental health needs and experiences of lesbians with disabilities exists, it is unknown how many of them are in need of, access, or are denied appropriate mental health services. The little research that exists on the mental health needs of women with disabilities has either excluded or ignored the particular experiences associated with lesbian identity. Like-

---

Corbett J. O'Toole is Director, Disabled Women's Alliance, Albany, CA.

Allison A. Brown is affiliated with the School of Public Health, University of Illinois at Chicago.

Address correspondence to: Corbett Joan O'Toole, Disabled Women's Alliance, P.O. Box 6008, Albany, CA 94706-6008 (E-mail: Corbett@disabledwomen.net).

[Haworth co-indexing entry note]: "No Reflection in the Mirror: Challenges for Disabled Lesbians Accessing Mental Health Services." O'Toole, Corbett J., and Allison A. Brown. Co-published simultaneously in *Journal of Lesbian Studies* (Harrington Park Press, an imprint of The Haworth Press, Inc.) Vol. 7, No. 1, 2003, pp. 35-49; and: *Mental Health Issues for Sexual Minority Women: Redefining Women's Mental Health* (ed: Tonda L. Hughes, Carrol Smith, and Alice Dan) Harrington Park Press, an imprint of The Haworth Press, Inc., 2003, pp. 35-49. Single or multiple copies of this article are available for a fee from The Haworth Document Delivery Service [1-800-HAWORTH, 9:00 a.m. - 5:00 p.m. (EST). E-mail address: getinfo@haworthpressinc.com].

35

wise, lesbian mental health research has historically overlooked disabled women's identity and experiences. Shared experiences and other similarities, such as discriminatory attitudes in the health service system, social stigma, and self-devaluation, are discussed within the context of disabled lesbians' compounded risk for mental health problems. Service access and barriers, key therapeutic issues, and cultural competency are discussed as additional issues that emerge when addressing mental health services. We also examine how lesbians with disabilities have proactively networked, caring for each other through informal supports within their communities, and have creatively developed their own strategies and resources. The paper concludes with a discussion of new efforts toward gaining visibility, successful strategies for mental health practitioners in addressing issues and challenges associated with providing care to lesbians with disabilities, and recommendations for further research. *[Article copies available for a fee from The Haworth Document Delivery Service: 1-800-HAWORTH. E-mail address: <getinfo@haworthpressinc. com> Website: <http://www.HaworthPress.com> © 2003 by The Haworth Press, Inc. All rights reserved.]*

KEYWORDS. Disability, women, lesbian, mental health, counseling, health services (access)

Lesbians with disabilities have a history of being excluded or overlooked as distinct or valued groups in our society (Brownworth & Raffo, 1999; O'Toole, 2000; Tremain, 1996). Although it is reasonable to suggest that there are mental health concerns shared by all lesbians, if not all women, this paper focuses specifically on mental health issues and community-based services for lesbians with disabilities whose disability is *not* primarily psychiatric. We contend that this group of women is at risk for mental health issues which often go unrecognized. Traditional sources of empirical information have not addressed disability and lesbians together, and more research is needed to examine the intersections of lesbians' and disabled women's mental health. A review of the literature reveals only anecdotal glimpses of hypothetical connections between these sub-groups, primarily based on scarce, but rich, narrative accounts in which disabled lesbians have written about their lives and experiences (O'Toole, 2000; Tremain, 1996; Panzarino, 1994).

Traditional western concepts of health often come up against the disability community's argument that "health" and "disability" are distinct constructs, each defined by world views and social forces that determine how biomedical or physical differences are recognized, classified and assigned value. Acknowledgment from within the health community that persons with disabilities can have the same range of health and well-being as non-disabled persons, or that one's "mental" health status is as integral to personal well-being as one's "physical" health status, has been slow in coming (Gill, 1999a). Surprisingly, the intersecting relationships or integration of identity statuses generally are not explored within women's, lesbian, or disability research (Brogan, Frank, Elon, & O'Hanlan 2001; Berkeley Planning Associates, 1997; O'Toole, 2000).

INVISIBILITY AND MARGINALIZATION

Lesbians with disabilities may be ignored because both sex and disability have traditionally been considered taboo (Olkin, 1999), or this may reflect (on a more insidious level) a tendency of our society to devalue and consequently overlook certain groups of people (O'Hanlan, Cabaj, Schatz, Lock, & Nemrow, 1999). Effects of invisibility are demonstrated by the non-existence of relevant mental health information for and about disabled lesbians, and for mental health professionals who provide them services (Olkin, 1999). Gaining visibility is a critical concern because the lack of academic inquiry into issues pertaining to disabled lesbians has a direct impact on funding and policies affecting the lives of these women. No data are available from which to estimate the proportion of women with disabilities who also identify as lesbian. Incidental data identifying either sexual orientation or disability are often collected in studies of women's health, but rarely are both.

The term "lesbians with disabilities" encompasses a diverse range of women. A major problem in researching lesbians with disabilities lies in the multiplicity of terms and their meanings. Like "lesbianism," inconsistency in the language of "disability" and consequential conflation of terms pose many challenges to policymakers and researchers, disallowing a uniform comparison of groups in many research traditions (Brogan et al., 2001; O'Toole & D'aoust, 1999; Solarz, 1999). A related concern expressed in literature on disabled women is the tendency to generalize and minimize disability in ways that dismiss the minority experience through assertions that because everyone has "differences," we all can be viewed as *handicapped* in certain settings (Brownworth & Raffo, 1999; Olkin, 1999; Tremain, 1996). Lesbian health researchers have addressed similar difficulties in defining the terms "lesbian" and "lesbianism" (Solarz, 1999). Diverse sub-groups within communities may not agree with, or adhere to, *any* one way of delineating groups. Nevertheless, even if categories and definitions remain arbitrary, overlapping, or conflicting, they are needed. To explore and refine our understanding of similarities and differences within and between groups we label groups in certain ways and we use specific group characteristics to generate ideas about which factors have the greatest effects on individuals' lives.

Disability is at its core a women's issue, and therefore inherently an issue of importance to lesbians. Over 20% of women and girls in America have a disability (Jans & Stoddard, 1999). Infants and children with conditions leading to lifetime impairment are more likely than ever before to survive into later childhood and adulthood. In addition, the past century has seen a dramatic increase in life expectancy for women. As the likelihood of survival over time increases and women continue to live longer, the population of women with disabilities will grow (Jans & Stoddard, 1999). *Emerging* disability for women will help shape what America will look like in the coming decades. Further, the care and management of people with disabilities is most often relegated to women–whether caring for themselves, an aging parent, a child, a spouse, a lover, or a close friend–and often includes caring for more than one person. Yet, like most issues particular to women, the gender dimension of disability remains underresearched and underfunded. Barile (2000) discusses the importance of advocating for and securing adequate funding for research and programs because policymakers cannot create effective models if they are not aware of the economic and social problems experienced by people with disabilities.

MULTIPLE IDENTITY ISSUES

The disability and lesbian communities have a shared history of inadequate social and legal supports (Gill & Brown, 2000; Gill, Kirschner & Panko-Reis, 1994; O'Hanlan et al., 1999; Rankow, 1995; Tremain, 1996). As Hershey wrote in response to the Matthew Shepard case and other hate crimes:

> When politicians and/or citizens craft laws designed to limit one group's civil rights or educational opportunities, our society takes a step back from the lofty ideals of Justice and Equality . . . an intolerant society just isn't a safe place for anyone who is considered "different." (1999)

For many lesbians or disabled women, forming an identity as a member of another similarly oppressed group provides valuable support and resources. Indeed, lesbian/queer women with disabilities have written about how they struggled with one of their identities (either their lesbian or disability identity) while embracing the other. Disabled lesbians may find opportunities to "come out" within some parts of the disability and lesbian communities independently. Identity management can be thought of as a skill developed by lesbians with disabilities to maintain a sense of control over their environments (O'Toole, 2000). In order to attract a sexual partner, or to obtain membership in the lesbian community, a lesbian with a disability must be able to "present" herself as a lesbian. Yet, there are few settings where it is acceptable (or safe) to be a disabled woman who loves women. In an effort to protect themselves, many disabled women do not easily disclose their private sexual behavior or label themselves as lesbians (O'Toole & D'aoust, 2000). Clare describes her experience of her disability identity in relation to queerness:

> Somewhere in there, my desire to pass as non-disabled–really to be non-disabled–reluctantly let go but at the same time left its mark. . . . Isolation and connection tug against each other. . . . I never feel this way about queer community. . . . My butchness, my love of dykes and queer culture, my gender transgressiveness all make my connection to queer community unambiguous. (Clare 1999, p. 134)

Disabled women often are perceived as either incapable of sexual relationships, or unable to manage them (Asch & Fine, 1988; Gill et al., 1994). Disabled lesbians, in particular, are not thought of as having the same range of sexual choices as either non-disabled women or heterosexual women (Corbett, 1994; O'Toole & D'aoust, 1999; Tremain, 1996). Like nondisabled lesbians, disabled women who choose women as sexual partners are routinely assumed to have accepted the only option available to them. Disability and chronic illness clearly affect the sexual relationship, financial stability, and plans for the future of lesbian couples (Axtell, 1999). However, the impact of a partner's disability, personal and social support networks, and adjustment to disability by the non-disabled partner, have not been studied. Similarly, no research has focused on lesbian relationships in which both partners are disabled. One of the most well-known examples of "tangled" intersections between disability and lesbian issues in relationships is the story of Karen Thompson who had to fight for many years to gain legal representation of her partner, Sharon Kowalski, after Sharon became disabled (Thompson & Andrezejewski, 1988).

EMERGENT MENTAL HEALTH ISSUES

Because of the lack of research, basic questions about the prevalence and characteristics of mental health issues for disabled lesbians remain unanswered (O'Toole & D'aoust, 1999; Saad, 1997). Studies involving people with disabilities and those focusing on lesbians independently document that discrimination creates an increased need for mental health services (Olkin, 1999; Gay and Lesbian Medical Association, 2001). Because of persistent discrimination in health services, women with disabilities often are faced with the dilemma of having to choose between allowing misperceptions to persist or exposing multiple stigmatized identities and risking denial of quality care (O'Toole, 2000). The experience of multiple minority statuses is believed to increase the risk for mental health disorders (Greene, 1994). Therefore, understanding how self-concept is affected by social stigma and how disability affects relationships with partners, family, and health care professionals is of key importance to mental health (Saad, 1997).

Depression, Stress and Suicide

Emerging research shows that women with disabilities have very high rates of stress and depression (DisAbled Women's Network, 1993; Gill, 1999a; Nosek, Howland, & Young, 1997). The risk for suicide is believed to be high for women with disabilities, but this issue is complicated because suicide can be masked or facilitated under more "acceptable" social pretenses, such as euthanasia. Older women with disabilities have engaged in what Osgood and Eisenhandler (1994) call "acquiescent suicide"–passively reacting to the loss of meaningful social roles by refusing to eat or take medication. New evidence suggests that psychosocial factors are strong indicators of disabled women's risk of physician-assisted death (Kaplan et al., 2000). This raises serious questions about whether disabled women are freely choosing assisted-death, and whether they would have the opportunity to withdraw from physician-assisted suicide if underlying depression had been acknowledged and treated (Gill, 1999b). If disabled lesbians come to believe messages from major societal institutions that their lives are undesirable and avoidable (e.g., as in disability campaigns which focus exclusively on "prevention" or "cure"), what does this mean for those who are (or were) unable or unwilling to *prevent* their impairment, and cannot be *cured*? Gaining an understanding of the insidious ways in which external prejudice and internalized devaluation affect mental health is critical to the development of effective mental health services for all women.

Abuse and Violence

Advocates and researchers document alarmingly high rates of abuse and violence against women with disabilities (Berkeley Planning Associates [BPA], 1997; Fiduccia, 1999; Tyiska, 1998; Nosek et al., 1997; Sobsey & Doe, 1991).

Likewise, some evidence suggests that lesbians are at least as likely as hetero-sexual women to experience adult sexual assault or rape (Brannock & Chap-man, 1990), and that sexual coercion may be as prevalent in lesbian relationships as in heterosexual relationships (Waldner-Haugrud & Gratch, 1997). However, there is no information about how many of these disabled women who experience violence or abuse are lesbian.

The lack of recognition by health care providers of disabled women's risk for abuse and violence; disabled women's daily contact with, or dependence upon, an abuser (e.g., spouse or family member, teacher, or personal atten-dant); lack of training for law enforcement officers in the identification and ap-propriate response to abuse; programmatic and attitudinal barriers to accessible services; and the consequences of ableism, heterosexism, and ho-mophobia, combine to place disabled women, and in particular, disabled lesbi-ans, at considerable risk (BPA, 1997; Fiduccia & Wolfe, 1999; O'Toole, 2000). Domestic violence shelters are virtually inaccessible to lesbians with physical disabilities, and even 10 years after passage of the Americans with Disabilities Act, facility directors do not perceive the need for change or to ad-vocate for improved access (Fiduccia & Wolfe, 1999).

Substance Abuse

Although substance abuse among disabled lesbians is unexplored, evidence suggests that disabled women and lesbians are independently at risk for sub-stance use-related problems (Ford & Corbitt, 1999; Li, Ford, & Moore, 2000; GLMS, 2001; Masuda, 1996). Olkin (1999) suggests that people with disabili-ties may have the highest rates of substance abuse of any minority population, estimated at over 25% compared with 10% to 12% in the general population (Substances Abuse Resources & Disability Issues Program [SARDI], 2001). Disability is associated with a number of risk factors for substance abuse such as lower education, poverty, and fewer options for dealing with family vio-lence (SARDI, 2001). Emerging evidence of high rates of substance abuse use by women with disabilities is believed to be closely associated with high rates of violence and abuse (Li et al., 2000; Masuda, 1996). The risk increases dra-matically as disabled girls transition out of elementary school (Ferrerya, 2001). Other risk factors may include enabling behavior and lenient attitudes by family and friends, constrained social opportunities, higher rates of parental alcohol abuse, and physical and attitudinal barriers to drug treatment programs (Olkin, 1999). Despite these risks, people with disabilities are less likely to en-ter or complete treatment due to compounded physical, attitudinal and policy barriers within service systems (SARDI, 2001). Further, mental health providers appear unwilling or unable to acknowledge that disabled lesbians are a high-risk group (Olkin, 1999; Fiduccia & Wolfe, 1999).

GAINING ACCESS TO MENTAL HEALTH SERVICES

Lesbians with disabilities are often denied access to mental health services because of disability-related physical, attitudinal, policy or programmatic barriers (Olkin, 1999; Brownworth & Raffo, 1999; Rehabilitation Research and Training Center on Drugs and Disability [RRTC], 1996). If accessibility is addressed at all, most mental health centers focus exclusively on physical barrier removal, in part because of assumptions that disability means physical impairment. Contemporary models of mental health care are based on a medical model in which disability is defined in terms of individual deficits and the ways in which people with disabilities vary from highly valued mainstream norms. The emerging minority or social model of disability takes into account societal forces and environmental influences affecting how individuals experience disability within a given society. The social model also removes the onus of responsibility and deficit from the individual, and places greater emphasis on social forces and perceptions that can be altered or modified (Gill, 2001).

Traditional mental health training generally does not assist providers in gaining insight into the constellation of factors that influence the everyday life of a lesbian with a disability (O'Toole, 2000; Olkin, 1999). Mental health providers are not exempt from the powerful influence of stigma and social stereotypes (American Psychological Association [APA], 2000) and may unknowingly perpetuate stereotypes of lesbians, of people with disabilities, or both (Olkin, 1999). Health providers' beliefs about disability affect how disabled clients are viewed–they are often surprised to discover that many disabled women are independent, self-directed, and fulfilled (Gill, 2001; Olkin, 1999).

Cultural Competence

The notion of cultural competence urges mental health professionals to examine aspects of diversity within a larger population, acknowledge existing disparities in resources and services, and develop the necessary skills for addressing the unique experiences shared by individual members of a cultural group. Disabled women and lesbians share many concerns and experiences yet have distinct cultural realities. *Integrated* cultural competence is key to developing successful mental health service models. Often approaches considered to be exemplary for non-disabled or non-lesbian clients are based on beliefs or experiences that are irrelevant or do not adequately address the distinctive experiences of a person with a disability (Olkin, 1999) or a lesbian. Gill (2001) summarizes the challenges in assisting health professionals to gain cultural competence in working with disabled clients:

> What health professionals perceive the key problem (functional limitation) is viewed by many disabled persons as insignificant compared to socially derived limitations. What they thought was a tangible problem in the individual is in fact abstract and complicated, requiring cultural, political, social and economic analysis. What they expected to address successfully through systematic application of their skills is a frustratingly entrenched problem that eludes fixing. When they thought they were helping, it could be said that they were participating in a system that has hurt and dominated disabled people. . . . When they thought they were supporting the client's goals, it could be said that they were in collusion with cultural pressures to be normal. (p. 8)

Mental health service providers need to recognize that they can learn a great deal about cultural issues from their clients. However, serious ethical concerns surface when women with disabilities are asked or required to "educate" mental health service providers about basic disability issues during paid counseling time (O'Toole, 2000). Therapists need to be able to integrate into the therapeutic process new discoveries about personal, professional and political factors that affect the lives of clients (Olkin, 1999). Mental health providers who avoid discussing issues associated with disability or sexual orientation send a powerful social message that being a disabled lesbian is a taboo or shameful aspect of the client's life. The American Psychological Association [APA] (1999) and the National Clearinghouse for Alcohol and Drug Information (Center for Substance Abuse Treatment, 1998, 2001) have published specific guidelines for mental health professionals who provide clinical services to certain underserved groups, including people with disabilities and the LGBT community. These guidelines recognize that lesbians with disabilities experience a wide range of challenges associated with both disability and sexual orientation.

Access and Barriers

Attitudinal access is a reflection of policy and of individual staff members who are responsible for providing services (APA, 1999; Brownworth & Raffo, 1999; Olkin, 1999; O'Toole, 2000; SARDI, 2001). Do mental health providers have the knowledge and skills to make lesbians and women with disabilities feel understood, safe, and welcome? If not, what is needed to change this?

Asking these basic questions can help mental health providers evaluate their cultural competence. Potential strategies for improving cultural competence include reading about lesbians with disabilities; discussing issues important for lesbians with disabilities; getting consultation from lesbians with disabilities; and making a personal commitment to learn more about the needs of lesbians with disabilities.

Policy service barriers are entrenched in the assumption that what works for a "normal" person is what's best for all people. Examples of how assumptions become barriers include the requirement that personnel have a driver's license (when what they really *need* is to be able to get to clients' homes); the requirement that clients must be seen only in the agency's offices (which may have specific physical or psychological barriers); lack of appropriate fee adjustments (or sliding scales that do not allow for the inclusion of disability-related expenses such as special transportation); and lack of funding for basic accessibility needs (e.g., sign language interpreters, ramps). Related barriers include the lack of information about disabled or lesbian clients; lack of knowledge by outreach staff; lack of written or electronic materials in accessible formats (e.g., Braille, large print, accessible Websites); and inaccessible consent forms (i.e., not easily or independently accessed and understood by the person receiving services). Although staff may feel uncomfortable asking clients directly about access issues, avoiding such discussions may perpetuate the perception that lesbians with disabilities are unwelcome in agencies that provide mental health services.

GAINING VISIBILITY

This paper has raised more questions than answers about the mental health needs of lesbians with disabilities. However, because of strong grassroots efforts in the past 25 years, lesbians and women with disabilities have become increasingly visible to each other, and to the lesbian and disability communities. This increased visibility has created new views and ideas about women's mental health. The proposed draft of the World Health Organization's new ICIDH-2 (2001) includes components of health and well-being based on body functions and structures, and on activities and participation. Functioning, as defined in this report, is a dynamic interaction between health conditions and environmental factors that facilitate or hinder the impact of the physical, social and attitudinal world. This greater recognition of "contextual" aspects of disability reflects an encouraging shift in policy paradigms and an increasing awareness of sociocultural and environmental aspects of health and well-being.

The American Psychological Association (APA, 1999) formally recognizes disability issues in a set of guidelines for serving a diverse LGBT community, and mental health practitioners are writing about services for people with disability and other diverse identities. In addition, a few researchers are beginning to investigate the intersections of lesbian and disability identities and experiences in their work. Cultural events also reflect this trend–sign-language interpreters and wheelchair seating have been common since the mid-1970s. For example, the Michigan Womyn's Music Festival has a disabled resource area (DART) and has made a concerted effort to include disabled lesbian performers. In her report of a recent study on disabled lesbians in relationships, Axtell (1999) writes:

> Participants described their community affiliations variously, but almost all seemed concerned with building communities . . . where they could be their whole selves. They described their community membership broadly including neighborhood, workplace, religious, ethnic, as well as disability and lesbian and bi women's communities. They described many factors that influence their participation in and identity with their communities. Structural barriers like lack of wheelchair accessibility, lack of childcare, and insensitive scheduling of events, as well as classist, ableist, and homophobic attitudes were among the factors described. This suggests that in facilitating the development of collective identity, community activists and cultural workers must remain mindful of the multiplicity of communities to which any one person belongs. (Axtell, 1999, p. 70)

National and international health research agendas and policies are beginning to change. In the United States, Healthy People 2010 (U.S. Department of Health and Human Services, 2000) includes a section on disability and secondary conditions that outline specific objectives that address depression, emotional support, life satisfaction, social participation, environmental barriers, and accessibility. Unfortunately, the unique concerns of lesbian, gay, bisexual and transgendered (LGBT) people are not formally recognized, and no comparable overarching goal or set of objectives was identified. In response to this omission, LGBT health organizations, including the Gay and Lesbian Medical Association (GLMA), developed the landmark Healthy People 2010 Companion Document for LGBT Health (2001). This document contains specific sections on mental health and mental disorders (GLMA, 2001).

As important as these developments are, they are not enough. For example, we are unable to reliably estimate the number of disabled lesbians in the U.S. or in other countries. Much of the available published material on disabled lesbians consists of anecdotal or personal accounts such as public letters from disabled lesbians or ethnographic interviews–rich information that is often ignored by researchers. Researchers are in a unique position to advocate for lesbians with disabilities by conducting studies that integrate the voices and experiences of lesbians with disabilities and what is known from existing research. Investigators need to learn how to build their research studies from within, rather than apart from preexisting community mental health and consumer networks. Studies on surviving multiple oppressions and on culturally specific barriers are still needed. More research is needed that focuses on self-esteem, multiple identities and social stigma, depression, stress, suicide, abuse and violence, substance use and abuse, and relationships of disabled lesbians.

Studying lesbians with disabilities can create new ideas that enliven research and challenge investigators to create new paradigms. Studying disabled lesbians offers many exciting opportunities–to examine multiple identity communities, to bring together seemingly disparate fields of scholarship, and to create a base for further research. As the knowledge base continues to grow, training and dissemination programs can be designed to target service providers who work with the LGBT or disability communities, as well as consumers and advocates. Existing programs can be modified to incorporate new information to increase access to needed services. Scholarly communities can encourage and invite researchers, community organizers, service agencies, policymakers, advocates and lesbians with disabilities to participate in collaborative mental health conferences and agendas. More research that focuses on lesbians and women with disabilities needs to be conceived not only in reference to, or in comparison with, the "norm," but in reference to themselves and the diversity *within* their own communities. Finally, the mental health community needs to recognize that the recommendations here reflect issues shared by most, if not all, women.

REFERENCES

American Psychological Association. (2000). *Guidelines for psychotherapy with lesbian, gay, and bisexual clients.* Website: *http://www.apa.org/pi/lgbc/publications/guidelines.html.*

American Psychological Association. (1999). *Enhancing your interactions with people with disabilities.* Website: *http://www.apa.org/pi/cdip/enhancing.html.*

Asch, A., & Fine, M. (1988). Introduction: Beyond pedestals. In M. Fine & A. Asch, (Eds.), *Women with disabilities: Essays in psychology, culture, and politics* (pp. 1-38). Philadelphia: Temple University Press.

Axtell, S. (1999). Disability and chronic illness identity: Interviews with lesbians and bisexual women and their partners. *Journal of Gay, Lesbian and Bisexual Identity, 4*(1), 53-72.

Barile, M. (2000). Understanding the personal and political role of multiple minority status. *Disability Studies Quarterly, 20*(2), 123-128.

Berkeley Planning Associates. (1997). *Disabled women rate caregiver abuse and domestic violence number one issue.* Berkeley, CA: Department of Education.

Brannock, J.C., & Chapman, B.E. (1990). Negative sexual experiences with men among heterosexual women and lesbians. *Journal of Homosexuality, 19*, 195-210.

Brogan, D., Frank, E., Elon, L., & O'Hanlan, K. A. (2001). Methodologic concerns in defining lesbian for health research. *Epidemiology, 12*(1), 109-113.

Brownworth, V.A., & Raffo, S. (Eds.) (1999). *Restricted access: Lesbians on disability.* Seattle, WA: Seal Press.

Center for Substance Abuse Treatment (1998). *Substance use disorder treatment for people with physical and cognitive disabilities.* Treatment Improvement Protocol (TIP) Series 29, Substance Abuse and Mental Health Services Administration, DHHS Publication No. (SMA) 98-3249. Website: *http://www.health.org/govpubs/BKD288/29b.htm.*

Center for Substance Abuse Treatment (2001). *A provider's introduction to substance abuse treatment for lesbian, gay, bisexual, and transgender individuals.* Substance Abuse and Mental Health Services Administration, DHHS Publication No. (SMA) 013498. Website: *http://www.health.org/govpubs/BKD392/index.pdf*

Clare, E. (1999). Flirting with you: Some notes on isolation and connection. In V. Brownworth & S. Raffo (Eds.), *Restricted access: Lesbians on disability* (pp. 127-135). Seattle: Seal Press.

Corbett, J. (1994). Proud label: Exploring the relationship between disability politics and gay pride. *Disability and Society, 9*(3), 343-358.

DisAbled Women's Network. (1998). *Violence against women with disabilities.* Toronto: Author.

Ferrerya, N. (2001). Living out loud: Building resiliency in adolescent girls with disabilities. Website: *http://www.disabilityworld.org/03-04_01/women/lol.shtml* [September 10, 2001].

Fiduccia, B.W., & Wolfe, L.R. (1999). *Women and girls with disabilities: Defining the issues.* Washington, DC: Center for Women Policy Studies.

Ford, J., & Corbitt, E.M. (1999, Summer). Substance abuse: A strong risk, often overlooked. *Window on Wellness,* 8-11.

Gay and Lesbian Medical Association. (2001). *Healthy People 2010 companion document for LGBT health.* San Francisco, CA. Website: *http://www.glma.org/policy/hp2010/index.html*

Gill, C. (2001). What is the "social model of disability" and why should you care? *IDHD Alert, 12,* 8-9.

Gill, C.J. (1999a). As bad as we imagined: Empirical evidence of stress and distress in the lives of women with disabilities. Presented (via video) at Promoting the Health and Wellness of Women with Disabilities, Centers for Disease Control and Prevention, San Antonio, TX.

Gill, C. J. (1999b). The false autonomy of forced choice: Rationalizing suicide for persons with disabilities. In J.L. Werth, Jr. (Ed), *Contemporary perspectives on rational suicide. Series in death, dying, and bereavement* (pp. 171-180), Philadelphia, PA: Brunner/Mazel, Inc.

Gill, C. J., & Brown, A. A. (2000). Overview of health issues of older women with intellectual disabilities. *Physical & Occupational Therapy in Geriatrics, 18* (1), 23-36.

Gill, C.J., Kirschner, K.L., & Panko-Reis, J. (1994). Health services for women with disabilities: Barriers and portals. In A. J. Dan (Ed.), *Reframing Women's Health* (pp. 357-366). Thousand Oaks, CA: Sage Publications.

Greene, B. (1994). Lesbian women of color: Triple jeopardy. In L. Comas-Diaz & B. Greene (Eds.), *Women of color: Integrating ethnic and gender identities in psychotherapy* (pp. 10-29). New York: Guilford Press.

Hershey, L. (1998). *Prejudice and hate violence must be confronted.* Website: *http://www.cripcommentary.com/prev98.html#10/15/98* [November, 2001].

Jans, L., & Stoddard, S. (1999). *Chartbook on women and disability in the United States.* Washington, DC: U.S. National Institute on Disability and Rehabilitation Research.

Kaplan, K.J., Lachenmeier, F., Harrow, M., O'Dell, J.C., Uziel, O., Schneiderhan, M., & Cheyfitz, K. (2000). Psychosocial versus biomedical risk factors in Kevorkian's first forty-seven physician-assisted deaths. *Omega–The Journal of Death and Dying (Farmindale), 40*(1), 109.

Li, L., Ford, J., & Moore, D. (2000). An exploratory study of violence, substance abuse disability, and gender. *Social Behavior and Personality, 28*(1), 61-72.

Masuda, S. (1996). *Safety network community kit: From abuse to suicide prevention and women with disabilities.* Toronto: DisAbled Women's Network.

Nosek, M., Howland, C., & Young, M. (1997). Abuse of women with disabilities: Policy implications. *Journal of Disability Policy Studies, 8*, 157-176.

O'Hanlan, K.A., Cabaj, R.P., Schatz, J., Lock, J., & Nemrow, P. (1999). A review of the medical consequences of homophobia with suggestions for resolution. *Journal of the Gay and Lesbian Medical Association, 3*(1), 25-40.

Olkin, R. (1999). *What psychotherapists should know about disability.* New York: The Guilford Press.

Osgood, N.J., & Eisenhandler, S.A. (1994). Gender and assisted and acquiescent suicide: A suicidologist's perspective. *Issues in Law & Medicine, Spring, 9*(4), 361-74.

O'Toole, C.J. (2000). The view from below: Developing a knowledge base about an unknown population. *Journal of Sexuality and Disability, 18*(3), 207-224.

O'Toole, C.J., & D'aoust, V. (2000). Fit for motherhood: Towards a recognition of multiplicity in disabled lesbian mothers. *Disability Studies Quarterly, 20*(2), 145-154.

Panzarino, C. (1994). *The me in the mirror.* Seattle: Seal Press.

Rankow, E.J. (1995). Lesbian health issues for the primary care provider. *Journal of Family Practice, 40*(5), 486-496.

Rehabilitation Research and Training Center on Drugs and Disability. (1996). *Substance abuse, disability and vocational rehabilitation.* Dayton, OH: Wright State University.

Saad, S.C. (1997). Disability and the lesbian, gay man, or bisexual individual. In M. Sipski & C. Alexander (Eds.), *Sexual function in people with disability and chronic illness: A health professionals guide* (pp. 413-427). Gaithersburg, MD: Aspen Publications.

Sobsey, D., & Doe, T. (1991). Patterns of sexual abuse and assault. *Sexuality & Disability, 9*(3), 243-59.

Solarz, A.L. (Ed.) (1999). *Lesbian health: Current assessment and directions for the future.* Washington, DC: National Academy Press.

Substance Abuse Resources & Disability Issues Program. (2001). *Substance abuse among consumers of vocational rehabilitation services.* Website: *http://www.med. wright.edu/citar/sardi.*

Thompson, K., & Andrezejewski, J. (1988). *Why can't Sharon Kowalski come home?* San Francisco: Spinsters Ink.

Tremain, S. (Ed.) (1996). *Pushing the limits: Disabled dykes produce culture.* Toronto: Women's Press.

Tyiska, C.G. (1998). *Bulletin.* Presented at the Symposium on Working with Crime Victims with Disabilities. National Organization for Victim Assistance (NOVA), Arlington, VA. January 23-24. Website: *http://www.try_nova.org/2a.html.*

U.S. Department of Health and Human Services. *Healthy People 2010: Understanding and improving health,* 2nd ed. Washington, DC: U.S. Government Printing Office, November 2000.

Waldner-Haugrud, L.K., Gratch, L.V., & Magruder, B. (1997). Victimization and perpetration rates of violence in gay and lesbian relationships: Gender issues explored. *Victims and Victimology, 12*(2), 173-184.

World Health Organization (2001). *ICIDH-2: International Classification of Functioning, Disability and Health* (Final Draft). Website: *http://www.who.int/-icidh.*

Psychological Distress
in African American
Lesbian and Heterosexual Women

Tonda L. Hughes
Alicia K. Matthews
Lisa Razzano
Frances Aranda

Tonda L. Hughes, RN, PhD, FAAN, is affiliated with the Department of Public Health, Mental Health and Administrative Nursing, University of Illinois at Chicago.

Alicia K. Matthews, PhD, is affiliated with the Department of Psychiatry, University of Chicago.

Lisa Razzano, PhD, is affiliated with the Mental Health Services Program, Department of Psychiatry, University of Illinois at Chicago.

Frances Aranda, MPH, is a research specialist, University of Illinois at Chicago.

Address correspondence to: Tonda L. Hughes, PhD, FAAN, University of Illinois at Chicago, Department of Public Health, Mental Health, and Administrative Nursing, Room 956-M/C 802, 845 S. Damen Avenue, Chicago, IL 60612 (E-mail: THughes@uic.edu).

The authors would like to acknowledge the Lesbian Community Cancer Project and the following members of the research team who assisted with instrument development and data collection: Ann Pollinger Haas (PI of the New York City Survey), Ellie Emanuel, PhD, Alice Dan, PhD, Mary McCauly, BA, Carrol Smith, RN, MS, Sheila Healy, MSW, LCSW, Susan Guggenheim, BA, Jackie Anderson, PhD, Kathy Hull, MA, and Karen Williams, MS. In addition, the authors are grateful to Drs. Ann Haas, Timothy Johnson, and David Henry who reviewed the manuscript and made suggestions for revisions, and to Lisa Avery, PhD, Roberta Cassidy, MS, and Sonja Nelson, MSW, who assisted in merging the data sets and with data coding and analysis.

[Haworth co-indexing entry note]: "Psychological Distress in African American Lesbian and Heterosexual Women." Hughes, Tonda L. et al. Co-published simultaneously in *Journal of Lesbian Studies* (Harrington Park Press, an imprint of The Haworth Press, Inc.) Vol. 7, No. 1, 2003, pp. 51-68; and: *Mental Health Issues for Sexual Minority Women: Redefining Women's Mental Health* (ed: Tonda L. Hughes, Carrol Smith, and Alice Dan) Harrington Park Press, an imprint of The Haworth Press, Inc., 2003, pp. 51-68. Single or multiple copies of this article are available for a fee from The Haworth Document Delivery Service [1-800-HAWORTH, 9:00 a.m. - 5:00 p.m. (EST). E-mail address: getinfo@haworthpressinc.com].

SUMMARY. Similarities and differences in indicators of psychological distress, risk factors for distress, and methods of coping were assessed in African American lesbians and heterosexual women. Despite similar rates of risk factors, lesbians reported more indicators of psychological distress and more frequent use of alcohol or other drugs in response to stress. In addition, findings reflect an overall trend toward higher rates of drinking, alcohol-related problems, and use of other legal and illegal drugs among lesbians. *[Article copies available for a fee from The Haworth Document Delivery Service: 1-800-HAWORTH. E-mail address: <getinfo@ haworthpressinc.com> Website: <http://www.HaworthPress.com> © 2003 by The Haworth Press, Inc. All rights reserved.]*

KEYWORDS. African American lesbians, sexual orientiation, psychological distress, mental health

A variety of economic and social conditions increase African American women's risk for mental health problems (Leigh, 1995). Poverty, which affects close to one-third of all African American women (U.S. Bureau of the Census, 1992a) and nearly one-half of female-headed African American households (U.S. Bureau of Census, 1992b), has consistently been associated with negative physical and mental health outcomes (Leigh, 1995; Hogue & Hargraves, 1993; Pappas, Queen, Hadden, & Fisher, 1993; Miller, 1989). Among African Americans, the damaging effects of poverty are further exacerbated by racial discrimination (Hogue & Hargraves, 1993; Miller, 1989; Moritsugu & Sue, 1983).

The factors that place African American women at risk for mental health problems emerge from a complex web of oppression. Racism and sexism are persistent, pernicious conditions from which American society continues to suffer. For lesbians, heterosexism compounds racism and sexism to triply oppress African American lesbians (Greene, 1994). Although African American lesbians are an understudied population, existing evidence suggests that they may be at particularly high risk for psychological distress (Bradford, Ryan, & Rothblum, 1994; Cochran & Mays, 1994; Dean, Meyer, Robinson, & Sell, 2000).

Factors hypothesized to increase rates of psychological distress for African American lesbians include the stressors confronted by African American women in general, the impact of heterosexism in the larger society as well as within the African American community, fear of rejection or withdrawal of support by families of origin, and lower expectation of support from the African American community at large (Collins, 1990). The often intense homophobia in the African American community is further compounded by racism within gay and lesbian communities (Mays, Cochran, & Rhue, 1993; Morales, 1989).

We were able to locate only two published studies that examined psychological distress in African American lesbians. In a large study of homosexually active African Americans (603 women and 829 men), Cochran and Mays (1994) found that women's mean scores on the Center for Epidemiologic Studies Depression Scale (CES-D) were higher than those of African American men overall, and as high as the scores of African American men diagnosed with AIDS (Cochran & Mays, 1994). More recently, Morris, Waldo and Rothblum (2001) examined racial/ethnic differences in predictors and outcomes of sexual orientation disclosure in a large sample of lesbian and bisexual women. In this study African American lesbians and bisexual women scored significantly higher on the Brief Symptom Inventory (BSI) than did their European-American counterparts. Support for higher rates of psychological distress among African American lesbians was also found in the National Lesbian Health Care Survey (Bradford, Ryan, & Rothblum, 1994). Analysis of data from subgroups within this sample showed that more African American lesbians (27%) than African American heterosexual women (16%) reported having attempted suicide in the past.

Although the above studies are important contributions to the literature on the mental health of African American lesbians, they have been limited by a methodological shortcoming characteristic of most studies of gays and lesbians, namely, the absence of heterosexual comparison groups. This paper reports data collected from lesbians and a matched sample of heterosexual women in two major urban cities in the United States. Similarities and differences in indicators of psychological distress, risk factors for distress, and methods of coping reported by lesbians and heterosexual women are described.

METHODS

Data were collected through the Women's Health Survey, a project initiated by the Chicago Lesbian Community Cancer Project (LCCP) in 1992. The initial purpose of the project was to collect data on physical and mental health status, as well as behavioral and environmental health risks of lesbians in Chicago. After data were collected in Chicago, the questionnaire was revised slightly and used to collect data in New York City (NYC).[1]

In both sites, a central aim of the survey was to include not only a diverse sample of lesbians in the community, but also a group of comparable heterosexual women in order to provide a context for interpreting the findings reported by the lesbians. Toward this end, each self-identified lesbian who participated was asked to give a second color-coded duplicate of the survey instrument to a presumably heterosexual female friend, acquaintance, or colleague who was presumed to be heterosexual and who had a work role (including student, homemaker, or retiree) as similar as possible to the lesbians' own. Using these procedures, a total of 602 women completed the survey in the two sites.

It should be noted that the recruitment procedures used in the two sites varied in ways that affected the demographic makeup of the respondents. In both sites, the research team relied largely on informal social networks and small social gatherings to reach subgroups of the lesbian population, rather than bars or large community events that have been more commonly used in surveys of lesbians. In the NYC site funding was available to pay recruiters to secure the participation of lesbians from hard to reach populations, such as racial minorities and older lesbians. Coming from the targeted communities themselves, these recruiters produced a lesbian sample for the NYC survey, which was considerably more diverse than has been obtained in other lesbian health surveys, or in the Chicago site in this study. Such diversity extended as well to the heterosexual women recruited into the survey by the lesbians, even though the sampling strategy was designed to control only for work role, and not race or age. Differences in procedures and population demographics resulted in different proportions of African American respondents in the two sites. In NYC, 72 (37%) of the respondents identified fully or in part as African American, compared to 37 (10%) of the Chicago respondents.

Although participants were recruited into the Women's Health Survey either by virtue of their self-identified lesbian status, or because of their presumed heterosexual status, each respondent's sexual orientation was ultimately classified on the basis of responses to two questions included in the survey instrument: (1) current sexual interest or attraction; and (2) sexual behavior in the year before completing the survey. Both questions included the following response categories: "only men," "mostly men," "equally men and women," "mostly women," and "only women." The question concerning sexual behavior also included the option, "I have not had sex in the past year." By summarizing the combinations of responses to these two questions, five categories of sexual orientation were created: lesbian, heterosexual, bisexual, and two categories of inconsistent responses regarding sexual attraction and sexual behavior (e.g., attracted only to women but sexually active only with men, or attracted only to men but sexually active only with women). Among the 116

African American respondents, 69 were classified as lesbian, 40 as heterosexual, and seven as either bisexual or inconsistent. These seven were omitted from the analyses presented here, resulting in a final sample of 109 African American women.

The questionnaire was divided into eight sections, covering a broad range of topics related to women's health. Analyses reported in this paper focus primarily on indicators of psychological distress, risk factors for distress, and methods of coping, including use of alcohol and other drugs. In addition, we also explored data related to relationships and social support.

DATA ANALYSES

Data analyses include descriptive and inferential statistics for relevant variables. For dichotomous variables, percentages, cross-tabulations, and chi square analyses were used to assess similarities and differences between lesbians and heterosexual women. Pearson product moment correlations and independent groups t-tests were conducted to identify significant differences in continuous variables. Because of the small sample size many of the relationships of theoretical interest do not meet the conventional criterion for statistical significance (alpha = .05). Because of this, and the exploratory nature of the study, relationships that approach the .05 level or that reflect overall trends in the data are also noted.

RESULTS

Sample

Table 1 summarizes the demographic characteristics of the 69 lesbians and 40 heterosexual women included in this sample. Summary statistics in this table reflect a high degree of similarity between the two groups, yet a high degree of diversity in the overall sample.

Both groups of respondents were somewhat older than those included in most lesbian health studies, with 59% of the lesbians and 54% of the heterosexual women over the age of 40. Although about half of both the lesbian and heterosexual women reported that they had completed some college, a substantial proportion of both groups reported having a high school education or less. Eighteen percent of lesbians and 21% of heterosexual women had advanced degrees. No differences were found between lesbians and heterosexual women on either age or educational level.

TABLE 1. Demographic Data: African American Lesbian and Heterosexual Women[a]

	Lesbians (N = 69)		Heterosexual Women (N = 40)	
	n	%	n	%
Age				
<30	8	(12)	6	(15)
31-40	19	(28)	13	(33)
41-50	27	(40)	11	(28)
51-60	10	(15)	5	(13)
>61	4	(6)	5	(13)
Education				
HS or less	23	(34)	12	(31)
Some college or BA/BS	32	(47)	19	(49)
Adv. Degree	13	(19)	8	(21)
Employment[b]				
Full-time	46	(67)	26	(65)
Part-time	11	(16)	1	(3)*
Unemployed looking for work	9	(13)	6	(15)
Retired	4	(6)	2	(5)
Disabled	2	(4)	2	(8)
Not looking for work	2	(3)	3	(8)
Annual Income				
< $10,000	6	(9)	6	(15)
$10,000-20,999	15	(22)	3	(8)
$21,000-35,999	18	(26)	12	(31)
$36,000-50,999	14	(20)	9	(23)
$51,000-75,999	12	(17)	6	(15)
> $76,000	4	(6)	3	(8)
Relationships[c]				
In committed relationship	24	(35)	18	(45)
Living with partner/spouse	18	(27)	14	(34)
Children living at home	17	(25)	17	(43)*
Lives alone	23	(34)	9	(23)

[a]n's vary slightly in some categories due to missing data
[b]Some respondents checked more than one employment category
[c]Relationship categories are not mutually exclusive
* $p \le .05$

The majority of both groups of women reported that they work full-time for pay (67% of lesbians and 65% of heterosexual women). Although the proportion of women reporting part-time work was relatively small, significantly more lesbians than heterosexual women were in this category (χ^2 (1) 4.77, $p = .03$). Only 4% of lesbians and 8% of heterosexual women reported that they were retired or unable to work because of disability.

The median annual income range reported by both lesbian and heterosexual respondents was $21,000-$35,999. Although more lesbians (31%) than heterosexual women (23%) reported incomes below the median, this difference was not statistically significant. The majority of lesbians (85%) and heterosexual women (80%) reported that currently they contribute more than half to their total household income. It is important to note that a substantial portion of both groups (42% of lesbians and 45% of heterosexual women) reported that their income was insufficient to meet basic needs.

Slightly more than one-third of the lesbians were in a committed relationship. This proportion is similar to that of heterosexual women who were either legally married or in a committed relationship, but not legally married. Only one lesbian reported being currently legally married. In addition, somewhat similar proportions of lesbians and heterosexual women were living with a spouse or partner. Fewer lesbians than heterosexual women had children living at home (χ^2 (1) 3.76, p = .04). Thirteen percent of lesbians and 26% of heterosexual women reported living only with their children (χ^2 (1) = 2.73, p = .10); 34% of lesbians and 23% of heterosexual women lived alone.

Psychological Distress

Three specific indicators of psychological distress were selected for these analyses: history of suicidal ideation and attempts, use of medications for mental health or emotional problems, and use of mental health therapy or counseling.

Suicidal ideation and attempts. Almost twice as many lesbians (47%) as heterosexual women (26%) reported that they had seriously considered killing themselves at some time in their lives (χ^2 (1) 4.77, p = .02). In addition, significantly more lesbians (40%) than heterosexual women (12%) reported one or more suicide attempt (χ^2 (1) 4.34, p = .03). Most of the suicide attempts in this sample occurred in adolescence or young adulthood, from ages 15-19 and 20-29 years, with only one lesbian reporting a suicide attempt during her 30s; no suicide attempts were reported after age 39.

Of the respondents who had attempted suicide, lesbians were significantly more likely than heterosexual women to cite sadness and depression (46%, 13%; χ^2 (1) 4.65, p =.03) and loneliness (24%, 0%; χ^2 (1) 4.36, p = .04) as reasons for having attempted suicide. Other reasons for suicide attempts were problems with family (21%, 7%; χ^2 (1) 1.57, ns) and problems related to sexual abuse (15%, 0%; χ^2 (1) 1.98, ns).

Use of mental health therapy or counseling. Slightly more than one-half of lesbians (54%) compared with 33% of heterosexual women reported that they had ever received therapy or counseling for an emotional or mental health problem (χ^2 (1) 4.86, p = .02). Lesbians and heterosexual women did not differ on rates of current therapy or counseling (16% vs. 15%). The most common reason for seeking therapy or counseling was feeling sad or depressed (50% of lesbians and 47% of heterosexual). Other commonly reported reasons included problems with family, issues related to self-esteem, and problems with spouse/partner. The only statistically significant differences between lesbians' and heterosexual women's reasons for seeking counseling were related to issues of sexual abuse (χ^2 (1) 5.25, p = .02) and sexual identity (χ^2 (1) 5.25, p = .02); 22% of lesbians and no heterosexual women reported each of these reasons.

Medication for mental health or emotional problems. Three times as many lesbians (16%) as heterosexual women (5%) reported that they had at some time received medication (typically antidepressant or anti-anxiety) for a mental or emotional problem (χ^2 (1) 2.69, p = .09).

Risk Factors for Psychological Distress

To better understand potential sources of psychological distress among African American women, we next examined four separate risk factors: perceived stress, emotional support, sexual abuse, and physical violence.

Perceived stress: When asked to rate their current levels of stress on a scale of 0 (none) to 3 (extreme), both groups of women reported moderate levels of stress (lesbians M = 1.95, SD = .64; heterosexual women M = 1.87, SD = .73). However, 16% of lesbians and 18% of heterosexual women rated their current stress as extreme.

When asked about specific sources of stress, both lesbians and heterosexual women rated money, job, and overall responsibilities highest. The only statistically significant differences in sources of stress were children ($t(73)$ = 2.18, p = .03) and sexual identity ($t(95)$ = -2.08, p = .04), with heterosexual women rating children, and lesbians rating sexual identity, higher.

Emotional support. Overall, responses of lesbians and heterosexual women to questions about the level and sources of emotional support in their lives were similar. Among women who were either married or in committed relationships, 71% of lesbians and 59% of heterosexual women reported that they received emotional support from their spouse/partner. The majority (74%) of both lesbians and heterosexual women reported receiving emotional support from friends. Fewer lesbians than heterosexual women reported receiving emotional support from their parents (23% vs. 39%, p = .07). When sources of support were summed, the average number of sources was similar for lesbians (M = 2.6, SD = 1.5) and heterosexual women (M = 2.7, SD = 1.9).

Sexual abuse. In response to the question, "Has anyone ever forced you to have sex that you didn't want?" almost one-half of lesbians (46%) compared with one-third (33%) of heterosexual women, reported that they had experienced forced sex in the past (χ^2 (1) 1.63, p = ns). Of the women who reported past sexual abuse, a significantly greater proportion of lesbians (35%) than heterosexual women (8%) reported sexual abuse by a male stranger (χ^2 (1) 3.99, p = .04). A similar, but nonsignificant, trend was found for abuse by a family member. Twenty-six percent of lesbians and 8% of heterosexual women indicated that a family member (i.e., parent, stepparent, sibling, uncle/aunt, or cousin) was the perpetrator.

Two lesbians (4%) and four heterosexual women (15%) reported ever being forced by a male spouse/partner to have sex. Similarly, three lesbian (6%) and three heterosexual (11%) respondents reported ever being forced by a male date to have sex. Three lesbians (6%) reported at least one experience of being forced by a female sex partner to have sex. None of the heterosexual women reported same-sex experiences of forced sex. Small and equal proportions (3%) of both lesbians and heterosexual women reported forced sex in their current or most recent relationship.

To assess rates of childhood sexual abuse (CSA), we asked women who responded affirmatively to the question about forced sex to indicate their age or ages at the time this occurred, using the categories "under age 5," "ages 5-9," "ages 10-14," and "15-19." Among the total sample, almost one-third (30%) of the lesbians compared with 18% of the heterosexual women reported having had such an experience before age 15. Because our response categories did not permit separating women who had experienced forced sex before age 18 (the more common definition of CSA) from those who had such experiences between ages 18 and 19, we were unable to assess rates of sexual abuse for women who were ages 15 to 18. Thus, the above percentages likely underestimate the number of both lesbian and heterosexual women who actually experienced CSA.

The importance of sexual violence/abuse as a risk factor for psychological distress was highlighted in additional analyses. Among lesbians, suicidal ideation was significantly related to a history of forced sex at any age (χ^2(1) 9.78, p = .002), as well as to CSA (χ^2 (1) 5.53, p = .02). In addition, history of forced sex also was related to lesbians' past use of medication for mental health or emotional problems (χ^2 (1) 9.82, p = .002). Perhaps in part because of the smaller sample size, only the relationship between history of forced sex and past use of medication for mental health or emotional problems was marginally significant (χ^2 (1) 5.18, p = .08) among the heterosexual women.

Physical violence. About one-half of lesbians (49%) and one-third of heterosexual women (38%) reported having been the victim of nonsexual physical violence at some time in their lives. Lesbians were slightly more likely to report past violence ($M = .93$, $SD = 1.20$) than were heterosexual women ($M = .55$, $SD = .88$) ($t(102)$ 1.71, $p = .07$). Of the women who reported physical violence, the majority (66% of lesbians and 87% of heterosexual women) indicated that the violence had occurred more than five years ago; 30% of both lesbians and heterosexual women who had experienced violence reported that they had been threatened or harmed with a weapon.

Family members were the perpetrators of physical violence reported most commonly by both lesbians (32%) and heterosexual women (22%). The difference between the proportion of lesbians (37%) and heterosexual women (17%) who indicated that a sex partner perpetrated the violence was marginally significant (χ^2 (1) 2.79, $p = .08$). Given the wording of questions, it was not possible to determine if the sex partner was male or female. However, 11% of lesbians (and 10% of heterosexual women) reported that they had experienced physical abuse in their current primary relationship, indicating that same-sex physical abuse did occur in at least a portion of lesbians' relationships.

Additional information about experiences of violence/abuse came from responses to questions dealing with spouses'/partners' verbally abusive or controlling behaviors. Similar proportions of lesbians and heterosexual women (33% vs. 31%) reported experiencing verbal abuse in their current relationships; 16% of lesbians and 10% of heterosexual women indicated that their partners had prevented them from participating in desired activities such as seeing friends, going to work, or seeking medical care.

Coping

To explore how these African American lesbians and heterosexual women responded to stress, we first examined their responses to questionnaire items dealing with general coping strategies, both positive and negative. We then looked more specifically at their use of alcohol and other drugs as a potential coping strategy.

Coping strategies. Survey respondents were asked to rate their use of each of several coping strategies on a four-point Likert scale ranging from 0 (never) to 3 (often). Positive coping strategies included talking/reasoning out the problem, confronting the problem, meditating or praying, exercising, or doing something fun. Negative responses included overeating, smoking, and drinking/using drugs. Percent agreement scores include dichotomous combined responses for "sometimes" and "often."

Similar proportions of lesbians (57%) and heterosexual women (64%) reported use of exercise as a coping strategy. Both lesbians (14%) and heterosexual women (5%) reported limited use of talking or reasoning out the problem, and only 3% of lesbians and 10% of heterosexual women reported confronting problems directly. Lesbians were somewhat less likely than heterosexual women to report using meditation and prayer (23%, 38%), but only "doing something fun when stressed" was statistically different for the two groups (17%, 38%; χ^2 (1) 5.21, $p = .02$).

No significant differences were found between the proportions of lesbians and heterosexual women, respectively, who reported using negative coping strategies sometimes or often, including overeating (50%, 46%), smoking (32%, 23%), or drinking/using drugs (19%, 13%). In each of these areas, however, lesbians evidenced a trend toward greater reliance on negative coping behaviors. In addition, when mean differences in frequency of use of the coping strategies were explored, frequency of "drinking or using drugs" in response to stress was greater for lesbians ($M = .63$, $SD = .97$) than for heterosexual women ($M = .28$, $SD = .76$) ($t(95)$ 2.00, $p = .05$).

Use of alcohol and other drugs. In this sample, 77% of lesbians and 64% of heterosexual women described themselves as current drinkers. Among current drinkers, almost all of the women reported light to moderate drinking (fewer than two drinks per day on average). Very few drinkers–6% of lesbians and 4% of heterosexuals–reported consuming more than two drinks per day on average.

A larger, but not statistically significant, percentage of heterosexual women (36%) than lesbians (23%) reported 12-month abstention from alcohol. Although we were unable to determine how many of the women were in recovery, 20% of lesbians and 10% of heterosexual women reported that they had gotten help for alcohol or other drug problems in the past. Few of the women who reported 12-month abstention also reported past help for an alcohol or other drug problem (27% of lesbians and 21% of heterosexual women). This suggests that most abstainers in this sample chose not to drink for reasons other than previous alcohol problems.

Responses to six alcohol-related problems, including feeling guilty about drinking, inability to cut down/quit, morning drinking, feeling annoyed by others' criticisms of drinking behavior, engaging in drinking behavior that negatively affects personal relationships, and drinking behavior that affected chances for a job or promotion were also compared. Despite similar and relatively low levels of alcohol consumption in both groups, almost five times as many lesbians (19%) as heterosexual women (4%) reported having experienced more than one of the six problem indicators in the past 12 months (χ^2 (1) 3.28, $p = .07$).

Table 2 summarizes rates of past and present (occasional and regular) use of several types or categories of drugs. Although there was a trend toward greater use of all categories of drugs by lesbians, only differences in past use of hallucinogens and opiates were statistically significant. Marijuana was the most commonly used drug; 27% of lesbians and 18% of heterosexual women reported past use. Fewer lesbians (12%) and heterosexual women (8%) reported current marijuana use. Close to one-fourth (22%) of lesbians and 15% of heterosexual women reported past use of powder or crack cocaine. None of the heterosexual women and only 4% of lesbians reported current use of crack or cocaine. The majority of both lesbians and heterosexual women reported hav-

TABLE 2. Past and Present Drug Use[a]

Drug	Lesbians N = 69		Heterosexual Women N = 40	
	n	%	n	%
Prescription tranquilizers				
Past	19	(27)	7	(18)
Present	6	(9)	3	(8)
Marijuana or hashish				
Past	18	(26)	7	(18)
Present	8	(12)	3	(8)
Cocaine/Crack				
Past	15	(21)	6	(15)
Present	3	(4)	0	(0)
Uppers/stimulants				
Past	7	(10)	2	(5)
Present	1	(1)	0	(0)
Downers				
Past	8	(12)	2	(5)
Present	0	(0)	0	(0)
Hallucinogens				
Past	8	(12)	0	(0)*
Present	0	(0)	0	(0)
Opiates (e.g., heroin)				
Past	8	(12)	1	(3)[a]
Present	0	(0)	0	(0)
Any Prescription Drug Use				
Past	42	(61)	25	(63)
Present	18	(26)	6	(15)
Any Illicit Drug Use				
Past	26	(38)	10	(25)
Present	10	(15)	3	(8)
Cigarette Use				
Ever	43	(63)	29	(76)
Current	25	(37)	9	

[a]N's vary due to missing data
*$p \le .05$, [a]$p = .09$

ing smoked in their lifetimes; more than one-third (37%) of lesbians and about one-fourth (24%) of heterosexual women reported that they currently smoked cigarettes.

To assess whether drinking alcohol or using other drugs might be used as a coping strategy, correlations between the response "drink/use other drugs too much" from the Responses to Stress scale, coded 0 (never) to 3 (often), and several of the risk factors were analyzed separately for lesbians and heterosexual women. Among heterosexual women, drinking or using drugs to cope with stress was significantly associated with level of stress ($r(38) = .40, p = .02$); history of forced sex ($r(39) = .53, p < .001$); CSA ($r(21) = .46, p < .001$); and history of physical violence ($r(39) = .50, p = .001$). Among lesbians, drinking or using drugs in response to stress was significantly associated only with number of alcohol problems reported ($r(53) .45, p = .001$).

DISCUSSION

Despite similarities in risk factors, lesbians reported more indicators of psychological distress than did heterosexual women in this study. For example, lesbians were significantly more likely than heterosexual women to report past use of therapy or counseling, and to report childhood sexual abuse as a reason for seeking therapy. In addition, more lesbians reported that they had taken medication for a mental or emotional problem in the past and were more likely to have used antidepressants. Whether these findings reflect greater psychological distress among African American lesbians than among African American heterosexual women, or whether they are related to lesbians' overall greater use of mental health services (and consequently higher rate of prescribed psychotherapeutic medications), remains unclear.

Although used as an indicator of psychological distress in this study, therapy or counseling can be a healthy method of coping with stress. African American lesbians in this study reported higher rates of use of mental health services than did their heterosexual counterparts, but these rates were substantially lower than the 78% to 80% rates reported for lesbians elsewhere (Bradford, Ryan, & Rothblum, 1994; Hughes, Haas, & Avery, 1997; Morgan, 1997). While data from studies of mostly white lesbians should not be viewed as "normative," differences in rates of mental health service use emphasize the importance of gaining a better understanding of African American lesbians' unique coping strategies, attitudes and beliefs about mental health and mental health services, and access to needed resources.

Findings in this study related to suicidal ideation and suicide attempts provide the most concrete evidence of psychological distress. Consistent with other studies in the literature (e.g., Bradford, Ryan, & Rothblum, 1994; Cochran & Mays, 1994; Hughes et al., 2000; Hughes, Wilsnack, & Johnson, in press), more lesbians than heterosexual women reported suicidal ideation and suicide attempts. However, like other studies that have analyzed such data by age, almost all suicide attempts were reported to have occurred when the lesbians were in their teens or twenties. This finding raises unanswered questions about whether, or how much, the reported suicidal behavior was associated with the "coming-out" experience, or to what extent it might be attributed to more general stress associated with being lesbian. Regardless of its cause, therapists and other mental health providers who work with lesbians and gay men should be aware that the risk of suicide may be elevated, particularly among young lesbian or gay clients or clients who are unsure of their sexual identity.

Use of alcohol and other drugs as a means of coping with stress has received widespread attention in the literature. The self-medication hypothesis is frequently used to explain research findings of higher rates of alcohol use and alcohol-related problems among lesbians and gay men (Hughes & Wilsnack, 1997). Although only a few differences between lesbians and heterosexual women reached statistical significance, the data showed a trend toward greater current use of alcohol and other drugs among lesbians. The rate of abstention from alcohol in the heterosexual group was higher (36%) and the rate for lesbians (23%) about the same as the 26% reported for African American women in a 1984 general population survey (Caetano, 1994). Despite similar and relatively low levels of current alcohol consumption, lesbians were three times as likely as the heterosexual women to report alcohol-related problems in the past 12 months and twice as likely to report past treatment for an alcohol or drug related problem. Although neither of these differences reached statistical significance, these findings are consistent with those of previous studies reporting higher rates of substance use and/or higher rates of problems among lesbians (Bloomfield, 1993; Hughes, Johnson, & Wilsnack, 2001; McKirnan & Peterson, 1989; Skinner, 1994).

Lesbians also reported more frequent use of alcohol or other drugs in response to stress than did heterosexual women. History of forced sex and CSA were associated with drinking or using drugs to cope with stress among heterosexual women, but not among lesbians. These findings differ from those of a more recent study conducted with a racially diverse sample of lesbians and heterosexual women in Chicago (Hughes, Johnson, & Wilsnack, 2001). In that study both adult sexual assault and CSA were associated with alcohol abuse among heterosexual women; however, only CSA was associated with alcohol abuse in lesbians. Lesbians' greater use of therapy, especially in response to issues related to sexual abuse, may help explain why we did not find a relationship between CSA and alcohol abuse in the current study. Among respondents who had been sexually abused as children, 69% of lesbians reported that they had sought therapy or counseling for this reason, but none of the heterosexual women who had been sexually abused as children reported that they had sought therapy/counseling to deal with CSA. This finding, as well as the finding that suicidal ideation was significantly related to past history of sexual abuse among lesbians (but not heterosexual women), emphasizes the importance of addressing sexual abuse when working with lesbian clients.

The literature suggests that minority clients who seek therapy or counseling are more likely to terminate treatment prematurely, often limiting the effectiveness of therapy. Swigonski (1995) points out that the ability of lesbians of color to cope under the worst conditions can mask their need for material support and act as a barrier to effective mental health treatment. Despite the "survival capacity" of women of color, mental health practitioners must not lose sight of or ignore indicators of psychological distress and unhealthy coping strategies, such as drinking/using other drugs or the overreliance on eating or smoking, which were reported by a number of lesbians in this study. In addition, given the higher rates of therapy use by lesbians overall, research that explores the potential mediating or moderating effect of this form of help on long-term coping and mental health outcomes should be undertaken.

Several limitations must be acknowledged when considering the findings from this study. First, lack of standardized mental health measures, especially of psychological distress, limits the conclusions that can be drawn from this research. Second, the small sample size and subsequent low statistical power is a limitation. Many of the relationships approached statistical significance and would likely have been significant if the sample size was larger, but relatively few reached statistical significance at the .05 level. In addition, the small sample size also made it impractical to adjust the alpha level for multiple comparisons. Third, the proportion of African American women included in the Chicago sample was considerably smaller than the proportion of African American women (and presumably African American lesbians) in the overall population of Chicago. Therefore, it is likely that the sample is biased toward African American women with higher incomes and higher levels of education. Lesbians who participated in the study are likely to be most representative of urban-dwelling women who are relatively "out" in terms of their sexual orientation. Finally, the sample is from two large urban cities–Chicago and New York City–a fact that may have influenced many of the study variables, including, for example, use of therapy or patterns of alcohol and other drug use. Each of these factors limits the generalizability of the findings. Results do, however, support previous research and suggest areas of clinical practice and research that need more attention.

CONCLUSION

Despite similar rates of risk factors, African American lesbians were more likely than their heterosexual counterparts to report past indicators of psychological distress, and lesbians more frequently reported use of alcohol or other drugs in response to stress. Furthermore, findings showed trends toward overall higher rates of current use of alcohol and other drugs and higher rates of alcohol-related problems. Other indicators of negative coping (such as suicide attempts) were much more likely to have occurred when lesbians were in their teens or twenties than in later years. In addition, the finding that more than half of the lesbians have sought mental health therapy or counseling may reflect healthy attempts to cope with life stress.

Many African American lesbians view race as a primary personal characteristic and sexual identity as secondary. Race often serves as a proxy for the influences of biology, culture, socioeconomic status, and exposure to racism (Johnson et al., 1995). The similarities between African American lesbians and heterosexual women suggest the powerful shaping influence–both positive and negative–of race on these women's lives. Nevertheless, given the indicators of greater psychological distress among lesbians, more research is needed to identify specific risk factors associated with multiple marginalized statuses. Such work is necessary to better understand whether race and sexual identity are additive, interactive, both, or neither in predicting psychological distress and mental health status. Until such research is conducted, the question of whether a lesbian identity increases African American women's vulnerability to psychological distress cannot be answered.

AUTHOR NOTE

Merging of the data sets and data analysis was supported by the Lesbian Health Fund, a Mental Health Services Research Grant on Women and Gender from the National Institute on Mental Health #1R24 MH54212, University of Illinois (UIC) Department of Psychiatry, and an Internal Research Support Grant from the UIC College of Nursing. The Chicago Board of Health and the Chicago Foundation for Women supported the Chicago survey. The New York survey was supported by a grant from the Professional Staff Congress of the City University of New York. Development of this manuscript was supported by a research grant K01 AA00266 (Tonda Hughes, PI) from the National Institute on Alcohol Abuse and Alcoholism and the Office of Research on Women's Health, National Institutes of Health.

NOTE

1. Data were also collected in Minneapolis/St. Paul, Minnesota. Because of the very small number of African American respondents, and because unlike Chicago and NYC, Minneapolis/St. Paul is not a major metropolitan area, these data were not included.

REFERENCES

Bloomfield, K. (1993). A comparison of alcohol consumption between lesbians and heterosexual women in an urban population. *Drug and Alcohol Dependence, 33,* 257-269.

Bradford, J., Ryan, C., & Rothblum, E. (1994). National lesbian health care survey: Implications for mental health care. *Journal of Consulting and Clinical Psychology, 62,* 228-242.

Caetano, R. (1994). Drinking and alcohol-related problems among minority women. *Alcohol Health & Research World, 18*(3), 233-241.

Cochran, S.D., & Mays, V.M. (1994). Depressive distress among homosexually active African American men and women. *American Journal of Psychiatry, 151* (4), 524-529.

Collins, P.H. (1990). Homophobia and Black lesbians. In *Black feminist thought: Knowledge, consciousness, and the politics of empowerment* (pp. 192-196). Boston: HarperCollins.

Dean, L., Meyer, I.H., Robinson, K., & Sell, R.L. et al. (2000). Lesbian, gay, bisexual, and transgender health: Findings and concerns. *Journal of the Lesbian and Gay Medical Association, 4,* 102-151.

Greene, B. (1994). Lesbian women of color: Triple jeopardy. In L. Comas-Diaz & B. Greene (Eds.), *Women of color: Integrating ethnic and gender identities in psychotherapy* (pp. 10-29). New York: Guilford Press.

Hogue, C.J.R., & Hargraves, M.A. (1993). Class, race, and infant mortality in the United States. *American Journal of Public Health, 83,* 9-12.

Hughes, T.L., Haas, A.P, Razzano, L., Cassidy, R., & Matthews, A.K. (2000). Comparing lesbians and heterosexual women's mental health: Results from a multi-site women's health survey. *Journal of Gay & Lesbian Social Services, 11*(1), 57-76.

Hughes, T.L., Haas, A.P., & Avery, L. (1997). Lesbians and mental health: Preliminary results from the Chicago women's health survey. *Journal of the Gay and Lesbian Medical Association, 1,* 133-144.

Hughes, T.L., Johnson, T., & Wilsnack, S.C. (2001). Sexual assault and alcohol abuse: A comparison of lesbians and heterosexual women. *Journal of Substance Abuse, 13,* 515-532.

Hughes, T.L., & Wilsnack, S.C. (1997). Use of alcohol among lesbians: Research and clinical implications. *American Journal of Orthopsychiatry, 67*(1), 20-36.

Hughes, T.L., Wilsnack, S.C., & Johnson, T. (in press). Lesbians' mental health and alcohol use: Research challenges and findings. In A. Omoto & H. Kurtzman (Eds.),

Recent research on sexual orientation, mental health, and substance abuse. Washington, DC: APA Books.

Johnson, K.W., Anderson, N.B., Bastida, E., Kramer, B.J., Williams, D., & Wong, M. (1995). Panel II: Macrosocial and environmental influences on minority health. *Health Psychology, 14,* 601-612.

Leigh, W. (1995). The health of African American women. In D.L. Adams (Ed.), *Health issues for women of color: A cultural diversity perspective.* Thousand Oaks, CA: Sage Publication.

Mays, V., Cochran, S., & Rhue, S. (1993). The impact of perceived discrimination on the intimate relationships of Black lesbians. *Journal of Homosexuality, 25,* 1-14.

McKirnan, D.J., & Peterson, P.L. (1989). Psychosocial and cultural factors in alcohol and drug abuse: An analysis of a homosexual community. *Addictive Behaviors, 14,* 555-563.

Miller, S.M. (1989). Race in the health of America. In D.P. Willis (Ed.), *Health policies and Black Americans* (pp. 129-189). New Brunswick, NJ: Transaction.

Morales, E.S. (1989). Ethnic minority families and minority gays and lesbians. *Marriage and Family Review, 14,* 217-239.

Morgan, K.S. (1997). Why lesbians choose therapy: Presenting problems, attitudes, and political concerns. *Journal of Gay & Lesbian Social Services, 6*(3), 57-75.

Moritsugu, J., & Sue, S. (1983). Minority status as a stressor. In R. Felner, L. Jason, J. Moritsugu, & S. Farber (Eds.), *Preventive psychology: Theory, research, and practice* (pp. 162-174). Pergamon Press.

Morris, , J.F., Waldo, C.R., & Rothblum, E.D. (2001). A model of predictors and outcomes of outness among lesbian and bisexual women. *American Journal of Orthopsychiatry, 71*(1), 61-71.

Pappas, G., Queen, S., Hadden, W., & Fisher, G. (1993). The increasing disparity in mortality between sociodemographic groups in the United States in 1960 and 1986. *The New England Journal of Medicine, 329,* 103-109.

Skinner, W.F. (1994). The prevalence and demographic predictors of illicit and licit drug use among lesbians and gay men. *American Journal of Public Health, 84,* 1307-1310.

Swigonski, M.E. (1995). The social service needs of lesbians of color. *Journal of Gay & Lesbian Social Services, 3,* 67-83.

U.S. Bureau of the Census (1992a). *Statistical abstract of the United States: 1993* (113th ed.). Washington, DC: Government Printing Office.

U.S. Bureau of the Census (1992b). *The Black population in the United States: March 1991* (Current population reports, Series P-20, No. 464). Washington, DC: Government Printing Office.

Self-Reported Sexual Identity, Sexual Behaviors and Health Risks: Examples from a Population-Based Survey of Young Women

Susan Scheer
Cheryl A. Parks
Willi McFarland
Kimberly Page-Shafer
Viva Delgado
Juan D. Ruiz
Fred Molitor
Jeffrey D. Klausner

Susan Scheer, PhD, MPH, is an epidemiologist, Seroepidemiology and Surveillance Section, San Francisco Department of Public Health, San Francisco, CA.

Cheryl A. Parks, PhD, MSW, is Assistant Professor, School of Social Work, University of Connecticut, West Hartford, CT.

Willi McFarland, MD, PhD, is Director of Seroepidemiology, San Francisco Department of Public Health, San Francisco, CA.

Kimberly Page-Shafer, PhD, MPH, is Assistant Professor of Medicine, University of California at San Francisco, San Francisco, CA

Viva Delgado, MPH, is Health Program Coordinator, San Francisco Department of Public Health, San Francisco, CA.

Juan D. Ruiz, MD, MPH, DrPH, is Acting Chief, HIV/AIDS Epidemiology Branch, California Department of Health Services, Office of AIDS, Sacramento, CA.

Fred Molitor, PhD, is a research scientist, Center for Health Services Research in Primary Care, University of California, Davis, CA.

Jeffrey D. Klausner, MD, MPH, is Director of STD Prevention and Control Services, San Francisco Department of Public Health, San Francisco, CA.

Address correspondence to: Susan Scheer, PhD, MPH, Seroepidemiology and Surveillance Section, San Francisco Department of Public Health, 25 Van Ness Avenue, Suite 500, San Francisco, CA 94102-6033 (E-mail: susan.scheer@sfdph.org).

[Haworth co-indexing entry note]: "Self-Reported Sexual Identity, Sexual Behaviors and Health Risks: Examples from a Population-Based Survey of Young Women." Scheer, Susan et al. Co-published simultaneously in *Journal of Lesbian Studies* (Harrington Park Press, an imprint of The Haworth Press, Inc.) Vol. 7, No. 1, 2003, pp. 69-83; and: *Mental Health Issues for Sexual Minority Women: Redefining Women's Mental Health* (ed: Tonda L. Hughes, Carrol Smith, and Alice Dan) Harrington Park Press, an imprint of The Haworth Press, Inc., 2003, pp. 69-83. Single or multiple copies of this article are available for a fee from The Haworth Document Delivery Service [1-800-HAWORTH, 9:00 a.m. - 5:00 p.m. (EST). E-mail address: getinfo@haworthpressinc.com].

SUMMARY. Data from a population-based survey of low-income young women (n = 2,438) was used to examine substance use patterns and exposure to coerced sexual activity among women who self-identify as lesbian (n = 34) or bisexual (n = 91), or who report sexual behavior exclusively with other women (n = 17) or with both women and men (n = 189). Findings for women classified by self-identity and by sexual behavior are compared. Women who identified as bisexual or lesbian reported higher rates of lifetime and recent substance use and were more likely to report experiences of coerced sex than women who identified as heterosexual. Women with both male and female sex partners reported higher rates of substance use and coerced sexual experiences than did women with male partners only. Heterosexual women with both male and female partners were more similar to self-identified bisexuals, compared to heterosexual women with male partners only. The implications of assessing multiple dimensions of sexual orientation in research focusing on lesbians' mental health are discussed. *[Article copies available for a fee from The Haworth Document Delivery Service: 1-800-HAWORTH. E-mail address: <getinfo@haworthpressinc.com> Website: <http://www.HaworthPress.com> © 2003 by The Haworth Press, Inc. All rights reserved.]*

KEYWORDS. Lesbian, sexual orientation, same-sex partners, alcohol use, drug use, sexual assault

Researchers examining health and mental health issues of women have generally taken one of two approaches to assessing or analyzing the sexual orientation of study participants. Most often researchers have relied on participants to self-identify as lesbian, bisexual, or heterosexual (Aaron, Markovic, Danielson, Honnold, Janosky, & Schmidt, 2001; Bloomfield, 1993; Bradford, Ryan, & Rothblum, 1994; Descamps, Rothblum, Bradford, & Ryan, 2000; Diamant, Wold, Spritzer, & Gelberg, 2000; McKirnan & Peterson, 1989a; McKirnan & Peterson, 1989b; Nawyn, Richman, Rospenda, & Hughes, 2000; Skinner & Otis, 1992), while others have classified participants according to the gender of their reported sexual partners (Cochran & Mays, 2000; Dean, Meyer, Robinson, Sell, Sember, Silenzio et al., 2000; Gilman, Cochran, Mays, Hughes, Ostrow, & Kessler, 2001; Hughes, Haas, Razzano, Cassidy, & Matthews, 2000; Marrazzo, Koutsky, & Handsfiel, 2001). Few researchers have assessed both sexual identity and sexual behavior. Moreover, relatively few studies have assessed women's sexual identity or sexual behavior with other women in representative or population-based samples (Solarz, 1999).

Findings from studies using both sexual identity and sexual behavior have shown that these two dimensions of sexual orientation are not always consistent (Diamant, Schuster, McGuigan, & Lever, 1999; White, 1997). Some women who have sex with other women do not identify as lesbian or bisexual, and women who self-identify as lesbian often report current or past sexual behavior with men. Thus, either approach alone risks the exclusion of important segments of the sexual minority population. Further, because many study samples are small and often homogeneous, researchers commonly aggregate women who identify as bisexual with those who identify as lesbian, or omit bisexual women from the data analyses (Aaron et al., 2001; Bloomfield, 1993; McKirnan & Peterson, 1989a). Similarly, women who report exclusively same-sex behavior may be aggregated with respondents who report sexual activity with both women and men (Cochran & Mays, 2000; Gilman et al., 2001), again potentially masking variability in the health and mental health issues of these groups.

Substance abuse and forced sexual activity, particularly within a context of limited economic resources, are recognized as important risks to the mental health and overall well-being of women. Research suggests that lesbians are at greater risk for substance abuse than are heterosexual women (Bloomfield, 1993; Hughes et al., 2000). In addition, lesbians may be more vulnerable than heterosexual women to some forms of forced sex and to the negative mental health consequences of sexual assault, in part due to the social stigma and marginalized status of sexual minorities within the majority culture (Descamps et al., 2000; Hughes et al., 2000). Understanding the experiences of self-identified bisexual women, or of women whose self-identity and sexual behavior are not consistent, has been constrained by limitations in existing research (Dean et al., 2000; Solarz, 1999).

We report findings from a population-based survey of low-income young women that asked participants about both sexual behavior and sexual identity. Information about demographic characteristics, alcohol and other drug use, and exposure to coerced sexual activity are described for women classified by self-identity and by sexual behavior. Similarities and differences between these two groups and between the two groups and heterosexual respondents are reported. The implications of assessing multiple dimensions of sexual orientation in research focusing on lesbians' mental health are also discussed.

METHODS

The Young Women's Survey (YWS) was a cross-sectional, population-based, household survey of women aged 18 to 29 years living in low-income census tract households in five Northern California counties (Alameda, Contra Costa, San Francisco, San Joaquin and San Mateo). The sample was recruited between April 1996 and January 1998. Within each county, census-block groups with median household income below the 10th percentile, as determined from the 1990 census data, were identified. Outreach teams identified eligible participants by enumerating household occupants in randomly selected street blocks during door-to-door encounters. Households were defined as any sheltered dwelling, including abandoned buildings with squatting residents. During the 21-month data collection period, 3,556 eligible women were identified and given the opportunity to participate; of these, 2,543 (71.5%) were enrolled. After informed consent was obtained, a 45-minute, face-to-face, structured interview was conducted with each participant. Counseling and referral information was provided as needed.

The primary objective of the YWS was to assess the prevalence of sexually transmitted diseases (STDs), including HIV infection, and to assess STD and/or HIV risk behaviors. Participants were asked about sociodemographic characteristics, medical history, sexual activity with male and female partners, history of sexually transmitted diseases, drug and alcohol use, knowledge of HIV/AIDS prevention methods, and use of health services.

The YWS protocol was reviewed and approved by the State of California Health and Welfare Agency, Committee for the Protection of Human Subjects. The study methods, study population, and primary outcomes have been described in additional detail elsewhere (Ruiz, Molitor, McFarland, Klausner, Lemp, Page-Shafer, & Parikh-Patel, 2000).

MEASURES

Sexual Identity and Sexual Behavior

Participants were asked if they identified as heterosexual, lesbian, bisexual, transgender or something else ("other"). In addition, participants were asked if they had ever had sex with another person. Sexually active participants were asked if their sexual partners had been men only, women only, or both men and women. Participants who reported sex with women were asked for the total number of lifetime female sexual partners and about specific sexual behaviors with women during menses (either her own or her partner's) in the last six months. Participants who reported sex with men were asked the number of lifetime male sexual partners, the number of male partners in the last six months, and about specific sexual behaviors with men in the last six months.

All participants were asked if they had ever received money or drugs in exchange for sex. In addition, participants were asked if they had ever experienced attempted or actual forced sex.

Alcohol and Other Drug Use

Use of alcohol and other drugs was assessed as "ever used" and "used in the past six months." Participants were also asked about injection drug use (including cocaine, crack, methamphetamine, heroin and ecstasy) in the past six months and during their lifetime (ever). Participants who reported any past injection drug use were scored positively on the measure of lifetime drug injection.

DATA ANALYSIS

Participants were grouped based on self-identification as lesbian, bisexual, heterosexual, or other, and by gender of their sexual partners. Demographic characteristics, substance use and experiences of coerced sex were compared based on (1) sexual identity (heterosexual with lesbian or bisexual identity) and (2) sexual behavior (male partners only with male and female partners) (see Table 1). Because the number of participants was sufficiently large we also compared findings for groups classified by sexual identity and sexual behavior (heterosexual with both male and female sexual partners and bisexual identity with both male and female sexual partners) (see Tables 2 & 3). The point prevalences of women reporting the selected demographic characteristics, substance use history and coerced sexual behavior in each of these groups were calculated using Stata software version 6.0 (StataCorp, 1999). Mantel-Haenszel Chi-Square statistics were calculated for these comparisons. Fisher exact test results are reported for analyses in which an expected cell contained less than five cases.

RESULTS

Sexual Identity and Sexual Behavior. Our analysis was restricted to the 2,438 women who reported being sexually active during their lifetime. Table 1 presents participants' self-reported sexual identity by gender of sex partners. Of the 34 (1%) women who identified as lesbian, 22 (65%) reported both male and female sex partners. Of the 91 (4%) women who identified as bisexual, nine (10%) reported male or female sex partners only. Sexual identity and be-

TABLE 1. Sexual Identity Among Young Women Who Reported Any Sexual Activity in Their Lifetime by Gender of Lifetime Sexual Partners

frequency (row percentages) [column percentages]	Male Sex Partners Only	Female Sex Partners Only	Both Male and Female Sex Partners	Total
Sexual Self-Identity				
Lesbian	0 (0%) [0%]	12 (35%) [71%]	22 (65%) [12%]	34 (100%) [1%]
Bisexual	7 (8%) [<1%]	2 (2%) [12%]	82 (90%) [38%]	91 (100%) [4%]
Heterosexual	2153 (97%) [97%]	1 (<1%) [6%]	73 (3%) [43%]	2227 (100%) [91%]
Other Identity*	72 (84%) [3%]	2 (2%) [12%]	12 (14%) [7%]	86 (100%) [4%]
Total	2232 (92%) [100%]	17 (<1%) [100%]	189 (8%) [100%]	2438 (100%) [100%]

* Other identity includes those who indicated other identity, don't know, or refused to answer the question on sexual self-identity.

havior were more consistent among the 2,227 (91%) respondents who identified as heterosexual; only 3% (n = 74) of this group reported having had female sex partners only or both male and female sex partners. Similarly, the majority of respondents (92%) reported only male partners; less than 1% reported female partners only. Of the participants who reported female sex partners only, two (12%) identified as bisexual and one (6%) as heterosexual. Of the 189 (8%) women who reported both male and female sex partners, 22 (12%) identified as lesbian and 73 (43%) as heterosexual.

Demographic Characteristics. Table 2 summarizes the demographic characteristics of the total study population and for the three comparison groups (based on self-identity, gender of sexual partners, and self-identity with gender of sexual partners). The women tended to be non-white (84%), less well educated than participants in most studies of lesbian health (44% had less than a high school education), and poor (58% had a household monthly income less than $1000).

There were no significant differences between bisexual women and lesbians on any of the demographic variables. The direction and the magnitude of differences between lesbians and heterosexual women and between bisexual and heterosexual women were similar (data not shown). For these reasons, and

TABLE 2. Demographic Characteristics Among Young Women Who Report Lifetime Sexual Activity by Self-Reported Sexual Identity and Sexual Behaviors

		Self-Identity[1]		Sexual Behavior [2]		Identity & Behavior[3]	
	Total	Hetero-sexual Identity	Bisexual or Lesbian Identity	Male Partners Only	Male and Female Partners	Heterosexual w/male & female partners	Bisexual w/male & female partners
	n = 2438	n = 2227	n = 125	n = 2232	n = 189	n = 73	n = 82
Race							
White	16%	16%	36%***	14%	42%***	49%	39%
African American	34%	34%	30%	35%	30%	29%	33%
Latina	37%	39%	11%***	39%	12%***	12%	10%
Asian/Pacific Islander	5%	5%	6%	5%	3%	4%	2%
Other	7%	6%	16%***	6%	12%***	5%	16%*
Household Income							
$ 0-499/mo.	23%	22%	29%	23%	23%	15%	30%*
$ 500-1000/mo.	35%	35%	28%	35%	30%	33%	27%
$ 1001-3000/mo.	33%	33%	31%	32%	38%	40%	32%
> $3001/mo.	5%	5%	8%	5%	7%***	11%	7%
Education							
< high school	44%	45%	28%***	46%	26%***	26%	27%
high school	26%	27%	18%	27%	21%	22%	24%
some college or more	29%	28%	54%***	27%	53%***	52%	49%

Group Comparisons: 1 Heterosexual identity vs. bisexual or lesbian identity
2 Women who reported sex with males only vs. reported sex with male & female partners
3 Heterosexuals with male & female partners vs. bisexuals with male & female partners
* p < .05 ** p < .01 *** p < .001

because the bisexual and lesbian subgroups were small, these groups were combined in subsequent comparisons with heterosexual women.

Women who identified as bisexual or lesbian were significantly more likely than heterosexual women to be white and to have had at least some college education; these two groups did not differ on household income. Women with

TABLE 3. Selected Health Risk Behaviors by Sexual Self-Identity and Reported Sexual Behaviors

Risk Behavior		Sexual Identity[1]		Sexual Behavior[2]		Identity & Behavior[3]	
	Total	Hetero-sexual Identity	Bisexual or Lesbian Identity	Male Partners Only	Male & Female Partners	Hetero w/ male and female partners	Bisexual w/male and female partners
	n = 2438	n = 2227	n = 125	n = 2232	n = 189	n = 73	n = 82
Lifetime Use of:							
Alcohol	79%	78%	96%**	77%	97%***	99%	96%
Speed	14%	13%	42%***	12%	46%***	48%	52%
Marijuana	52%	50%	82%***	49%	89%***	93%	85%
Cocaine	16%	14%	43%***	13%	52%***	59%	52%
Heroin	4%	3%	20%***	3%	24%***	30%	24%
Injected Drugs	4%	3%	22%***	2%	24%***	25%	29%
Use in past 6 months:							
Alcohol	57%	56%	82%***	55%	83%***	81%	83%
Speed	5%	4%	26%***	4%	25%***	19%	34%*
Marijuana	32%	31%	62%***	30%	65%***	64%	67%
Cocaine	7%	6%	26%***	5%	24%***	23%	32%
Heroin	2%	1%	12%***	1%	11%***	7%	17%
Coerced Sex							
Traded for money or drugs	9%	8%	34%***	7%	38%***	37%	44%
Threatened with force	27%	25%	55%***	24%	60%***	63%	60%
Forced to have sex	25%	23%	50%***	23%	53%***	55%	55%

Group Comparisons: 1 Heterosexual identity vs. bisexual or lesbian identity
2 Women who reported sex with males only vs. reported sex with male & female partners
3 Heterosexuals with male & female partners vs. bisexuals with male & female partners
* p < .05 ** p < .01 *** p < .001

both male and female sex partners were significantly more likely than women with male only partners to be white, have incomes over $3000, and to have completed at least some college. Finally, we compared women based on sexual identity and gender of sex partners. Bisexual women with both male and female sex partners were more likely than heterosexual women with both male and female partners to report their race as "other" and to have monthly household incomes less than $500. Comparisons between heterosexual women with male partners only and those with both male and female partners showed the same pattern of demographic differences as comparisons using sexual behavior alone. That is, heterosexual women with both male and female partners were more likely than heterosexual women with male partners only to be white, to have completed some college, and to have a household income over $3000 (data not shown).

Mental Health Risk Behaviors. Table 3 summarizes findings related to several mental health risk behaviors for the three groups. Bisexuals/lesbians were significantly more likely than heterosexual women to report lifetime and recent use of all categories of alcohol and other drugs. Bisexuals/lesbians were also more likely to report having experienced coerced sex. Bisexual women were more likely than lesbians to report lifetime use of amphetamines ("speed") (51% vs. 21%; $\chi^2 = 9.0$, p = .002) and cocaine (51% vs. 24%; $\chi^2 = 7.3$, p = .006) as well as use in the last six months of heroin (15% vs. 3%; $\chi^2 = 3.6$, p = .05) and cocaine (31% vs. 12%; $\chi^2 = 4.7$, p = .03). Bisexual women were also significantly more likely than lesbians to report trading sex for money or drugs (41% vs. 18%; $\chi^2 = 5.8$, p = .02). Differences in threats of forced sex (58% vs. 47%; $\chi^2 = 1.2$, p = .26) and actual forced sex (54% vs. 41%; $\chi^2 = 1.6$, p = .21) were not significant. Women with both male and female sex partners reported significantly higher rates of alcohol and other drug use and coerced sexual experiences than women with male partners only.

A comparison of groups by gender of their sexual partners alone revealed significantly higher rates of alcohol and drug use and coerced sexual experiences among women reporting sexual activity with both male and female partners versus those reporting sex with men only.

Finally, with the exception of use of speed in the past six months, heterosexual women with both male and female sex partners did not differ significantly from bisexual women with both male and female partners on any of the health risk behaviors. Reports of health risks for heterosexual women with both male and female partners were more similar to bisexual women with male and female partners than to heterosexual women with male partners only (data not shown).

DISCUSSION

The Young Women's Survey was conducted to examine the sexual and health risk behaviors of low-income, young women living in selected counties in California. Both sexual identity and sexual behaviors of respondents were assessed. Data from this population-based study supports earlier research findings indicating that sexual identity and sexual behaviors are not always consistent (Diamant et al., 1999; White, 1997), and provided an opportunity to compare health and mental health risk factors based on women's sexual behavior and sexual identity.

Initial analyses of respondents grouped according to self-identity revealed findings that support, in part, earlier research on substance use. Consistent with some previous studies (Bradford et al., 1994; McKirnan & Peterson, 1989a; Skinner & Otis, 1992), women who identified as bisexual or lesbian reported significantly higher rates of lifetime and recent substance use than did heterosexually identified women. However, these findings fail to support more recent findings that lesbians are more likely than heterosexual women to abstain from alcohol consumption (Hughes et al., 2000), as well as suggestions that there is a growing "recovery consciousness" among select populations (Bloomfield, 1993). These inconsistencies may be explained in part by the limited measures of substance use (ever and past six months); demographic differences between this study population and earlier study populations (our sample was younger, more economically disadvantaged, and more racially diverse); and the greater proportion of bisexually identified women in our sample. Although we found significant differences between lesbian and bisexual women in only four drug-use categories, there was an overall trend toward higher rates of lifetime and recent substance use among bisexual women.

A question underlying this analysis was whether the definition of sexual identity used in studies and outreach efforts might exclude some women who are at risk for mental health problems. Our findings suggest that this is a realistic concern, especially in regard to substance use. Regardless of self-identity, women who had both male and female sex partners reported similar substance use histories. This suggests that sexual behavior may be more predictive of lifetime substance use than sexual identity. Thus, research or outreach focused on identity alone could result in the exclusion of a substantial proportion of women who might benefit from substance abuse education or treatment.

Victimization due to coerced or forced sexual activity places all women at risk for serious mental health consequences including depression, anxiety, self-destructive behavior and substance abuse (Descamps et al., 2000). In the present study, victimization was assessed using three questions that asked whether the respondent had ever (1) *traded* sex for drugs or money, (2) been *threatened* with force to engage in sex, or (3) been *forced* to engage in sexual activity. Significantly higher rates on all three measures of victimization were reported by bisexual women and lesbians compared to heterosexual women, and by women with both male and female partners compared to those with male partners only. Bisexual women reported higher rates of victimization than did lesbians (although only the difference in trading sex for drugs or money was statistically significant). In comparisons of groups using both sexual identity and behavior, heterosexual women with both male and female sex partners were slightly more likely to report *threats* of force than were bisexual women with both male and female sex partners. Rates of *forced* sexual activity were identical for these two groups. Overall, women who had both male and female sex partners reported higher rates of all three victimization experiences than did women who reported having had only male sex partners.

Measures of sexual victimization used in this study differ from those in studies of sexual assault reported elsewhere (Bradford et al., 1994; Descamps et al., 2000; Hughes et al., 2000; Hughes, Johnson, & Wilsnack, 2001); thus, our findings cannot be readily compared with those from other studies. Rates of adult sexual assault among lesbians range from 15% to 39%, depending on the characteristics of the study population (Bradford et al., 1994; Descamps et al., 2000; Dean et al., 2000; Hughes et al., 2001). Rates of sexual victimization for heterosexual women in this study (8% to 25%) were somewhat comparable; however, rates for lesbian and bisexual women (34% to 55%) are somewhat higher. Hughes et al. (2000) asked heterosexual women and lesbians if they had ever been forced by a male spouse/partner, male date, or female partner/spouse/date to have sex. Affirmative responses ranged from 1% (lesbians by a female date) to 17% (heterosexuals by a male date), rates also much lower than those reported here. However, because we did not ask about gender of the perpetrator of the coercive act, it is difficult to make comparisons.

Despite the lack of comparability in measures, our study findings suggest that sexual victimization is common among this population of young, economically disadvantaged and racially diverse women; young women who identify as bisexual or lesbian or who have sex with both men and women may be at particularly high risk. The similarity in rates of victimization reported by women with both male and female partners, regardless of self-identity, suggests the importance of using multiple definitions of sexual identification in outreach and research with sexual minority populations. Nevertheless, the choice of definition should be made within the context of the research questions, aims of the study, and planned health prevention strategies. Using sexual identity or sexual behavior alone may result in a lost opportunity to assess the health, mental health and general well-being of certain segments of sexual minority populations. For example, previous analyses of data from this study found that women who reported sex with both men and women reported significantly higher rates of sexual and injection drug-risk behaviors than women whose partners were exclusively male or female (Scheer, Peterson, Shafer, Delgado, Gleghorn, Ruiz, Molitor, McFarland, 2002). Analyses using sexual identity would have underestimated risk for HIV because many of the women who identified as lesbian reported current or past sex with men. In addition, information about sexual behavior is important when making recommendations for Papanicolaou (Pap) smears or when screening for sexually transmitted diseases, regardless of current sexual identity.

In other contexts, the gender of sex partners may not be of primary interest. For example, Avery, Hellman and Sudderth (2001) found that both lesbian and bisexual women were more likely than heterosexual women to express dissatisfaction with mental health services. These authors suggest that lesbian and bisexual women may benefit from services that target their particular needs. Further, some health prevention efforts using sexual identity alone have proven to be effective in appealing to and reaching both lesbians and bisexual women (San Francisco HIV Prevention Plan, 1997). Finally, both bisexual women and lesbians have identified discrimination and fear of stigmatization as obstacles to help-seeking and to receiving quality health care, including mental health services (Dean et al., 2000; Lehmann, Lehmann, & Kelly, 1998; O'Hanlan, Cabaj, Schatz, Lock, & Nemrow, 1997). Thus, when the focus is on barriers to treatment or addressing the unique concerns attributable to stigma and oppression, sexual identity may be more salient than sexual behavior.

As in the present study, use of multiple definitions of sexual orientation is often warranted. Our findings suggest that whether classified by sexual identity or by sexual behavior, participants reported high rates of substance use and sexual victimization. Had only sexual identity been used, a substantial proportion of women for whom the study aims are relevant would have been omitted. On the other hand, use of the sexual behavior alone may not convey the same degree of acceptance and inclusion needed to engage a population that has historically suffered oppressive and discriminatory practices.

Findings from our study must be interpreted in light of several limitations. First, we were unable to assess if women who reported lifetime female sexual partners were currently sexually active with women. Questions about sexual behavior in the previous six months were asked only of women who had sex with other women if they reported sex during menses. Therefore, some women classified as having female sex partners only, or both female and male partners, may have been exclusively sexual with male or female partners at the time of the interview. In addition, underreporting by respondents may have occurred, as some women may have been reluctant to discuss their sexual identity or same-sex behavior during a face-to-face interview. However, although the numbers of bisexual and lesbian identified women in our study was small, the proportion of women identifying as lesbian (1%) or as bisexual (4%) falls within a recent estimate of the proportion of the U.S. female population that is homosexual (1% to 3.6%) (Laumann, Gagnon, Michael, & Michaels, 1994).

Despite these limitations, this population-based study provides important information about a segment of the bisexual/lesbian population that has generally not been included in previous research. Further, it demonstrates the importance of the approach used to classify sexual orientation among study participants. In many studies, assessment of both sexual identity and sexual behavior is warranted. Given the inconsistency between sexual identity and sexual behavior, it is important to carefully craft questions that accurately capture both current and past sexual behavior as well as current sexual identity. Our findings support other studies that report a high prevalence of sexual and drug risk behaviors among women who have sex with other women (Bevier, Chiasson, Hefferman, & Castro, 1995; Einhorn & Polgar, 1994; Gonzales, Washienko, Krone, Chapman, Arredondo, Huckeba, & Downer, 1999; Lemp, Jones, Kellogg, Nieri, Anderson, Withum, & Katz, 1995) as well as findings suggesting that young, poor, lesbians of color are more likely to have had male partners in the past year. In addition, women who have both female and male sex partners may have more health risks than women whose sexual partners are exclusively male or female.

REFERENCES

Aaron, D.J., Markovic, N., Danielson, M.E., Honnold, J.A., Janosky, J.E., & Schmidt, N.J. (2001). Behavioral risk factors for disease and preventive health practices among lesbians. *American Journal of Public Health, 91* (6), 972-975.

Avery, A.M., Hellman, R.E., & Sudderth, L.K. (2001). Satisfaction with mental health services among sexual minorities with major mental illness. *American Journal of Public Health, 91*(6), 990.

Bevier, P.J., Chiasson, M.A., Hefferman, R.T., & Castro, K.G. (1995). Women at a sexually transmitted disease clinic who reported same-sex contact: Their HIV seroprevalence and risk behaviors. *American Journal of Public Health, 85* (10), 1366-1371.

Bloomfield, K. (1993). A comparison of alcohol consumption between lesbians and heterosexual women in an urban population. *Drug and Alcohol Dependence, 33*(3), 257-269.

Bradford, J., Ryan, C., & Rothblum, E.D. (1994). National lesbian health care survey: Implications for mental health care. *Journal of Consulting and Clinical Psychology, 62*(2), 228-242.

Cochran, S.D., & Mays, V.M. (2000). Relation between psychiatric syndromes and behaviorally defined sexual orientation in a sample of the US population. *American Journal of Epidemiology, 151* (5), 516-523.

Dean, L., Meyer, I.H., Robinson, K., Sell, R.L, Sember, R., Silenzio, V.M.B. et al. (2000). Lesbian, gay, bisexual, and transgender health: Findings and concerns. *Journal of the Gay and Lesbian Medical Association, 4* (3), 101-151.

Descamps, M.J., Rothblum, E., Bradford, J., & Ryan, C. (2000). Mental health impact of child sexual abuse, rape, intimate partner violence, and hate crimes in the National Lesbian Health Care Survey. *Journal of Gay & Lesbian Social Services, 11* (1), 27-55.

Diamant, A.L., Schuster, M.A., McGuigan, K., & Lever, J. (1999). Lesbians' sexual history with men. *Archives of Internal Medicine, 159*, 2730-2736.

Diamant, A.L., Wold, C., Spritzer, K., & Gelberg, L. (2000). Health behaviors, health status, and access to and use of health care. *Archives of Family Medicine, 9*, 1043-1051.

Einhorn, L., & Polgar, P. (1994). HIV-risk behavior among lesbians and bisexual women. *AIDS Education and Prevention, 6*(6), 514-523.

Gilman, S.E., Cochran, S.D., Mays, V.M., Hughes, M., Ostrow, D., & Kessler, R.C. (2001). Risk of psychiatric disorders among individuals reporting same-sex sexual partners in the National Comorbidity Survey. *American Journal of Public Health, 91*(6), 933-939.

Gonzales, V., Washienko, K.M., Krone, M.R., Chapman, L.I., Arredondo, E.M., Huckeba, H.J., & Downer, A. (1999). Sexual and drug-use risk factors for HIV and STDs: A Comparison of women with and without bisexual experiences. *American Journal of Public Health, 89*(12), 1841-1846.

Hughes, T.L., Haas, A.P., Razzano, L., Cassidy, R., & Matthews, A. (2000). Comparing lesbians' and heterosexual women's mental health: A multi-site survey. *Journal of Gay & Lesbian Social Services, 11*(1), 57-76.

Hughes, T. L., Johnson, T., & Wilsnack, S.C. (2001). Sexual assault and alcohol abuse: A comparison of lesbian and heterosexual women. *Journal of Substance Abuse, 13*, 515-532.

Laumann, E.O., Gagnon, J.H., Michael, R.T., & Michaels, S. (1994). *The social organization of sexuality: Sexual practices in the United States.* Chicago, IL: University of Chicago Press.

Lehmann, J.B., Lehmann, C.U., & Kelly, P.J. (1998). Development and health care needs of lesbians. *Journal of Women's Health, 7*(3), 379-387.

Lemp, G.F., Jones, M., Kellogg, T.A., Nieri, G.N., Anderson, L., Withum, D., & Katz, M. (1995). HIV seroprevalence and risk behaviors among lesbians and bisexual women in San Francisco and Berkeley, California. *American Journal of Public Health, 85*,1549-1552.

Marrazzo, J.M., Koutsky, L.A., & Handsfield, H.H. (2001). Characteristics of female sexually transmitted disease clinic clients who report same-sex behaviour. *International Journal of STD & AIDS, 12*, 41-46.

McKirnan, D.J., & Peterson, P.L. (1989a). Alcohol and drug use among homosexual men and women: Epidemiology and population characteristics. *Addictive Behaviors, 14*, 545-553.

McKirnan, D.J., & Peterson, P.L. (1989b). Psychosocial and cultural factors in alcohol and drug abuse: An anlysis of a homosexual community. *Addictive Behaviors, 14*, 555-563.

Nawyn, S.J., Richman, J.A., Rospenda, K.M., & Hughes, T.L. (2000). Sexual identity and alcohol-related outcomes: Contributions of workplace harassment. *Journal of Substance Abuse, 11*(3), 289-304.

O'Hanlan, K.A., Cabaj, R.P., Schatz, B., Lock, J., & Nemrow, P. (1997). A review of the medical consequences of homophobia with suggestions for resolution. *Journal of the Gay and Lesbian Medical Association, 1*(1), 25-39.

Ruiz, J.D., Molitor, F., McFarland, W., Klausner, J., Lemp, G., Page-Shafer, K., & Parikh-Patel, A. (2000). Prevalence of HIV infection, sexually transmitted diseases, and hepatitis and related risk behavior in young women living in low-income neighborhoods of northern California. *Western Journal of Medicine, 172*(6), 368-73.

San Francisco HIV Prevention Plan. (1997). HIV Prevention Planning Council, Department of Public Health AIDS Office, and Harder & Company Community Research. San Francisco, CA.

Scheer, S., Peterson, I., Shafer, K.P., Delgado, V., Gleghorn, A., Ruiz, J., Molitor, F., & McFarland, W. (2002). Sex and drug use behavior among women who have sex with both women and men: Results of a population-based survey. *American Journal of Public Health, 92* (7), 1110-1112.

Skinner, W.F., & Otis, M.D. (1992). Drug use among lesbian and gay people: Findings, research design, insights, and policy issues from the Trilogy Project. In *The Research Symposium on Alcohol and Other Drug Problem Prevention Among Lesbians and Gay Men* (pp. 34-60). Sacramento, CA: EMT Group, Inc.

Solarz, A.L. (Ed.) (1999). *Lesbian health: Current assessment and directions for the future.* Washington DC: National Academy Press.

StataCorp (1999). *Stata Statistical Sofware: Release 6.0.* College Station, TX: Stata Corporation.

White, J.C. (1997). HIV risk assessment and prevention in lesbians and women who have sex with women: Practical information for clinicians. *Health Care for Women International, 18*, 127-138.

Identity, Stigma Management, and Well-Being: A Comparison of Lesbians/Bisexual Women and Gay/Bisexual Men

Riia K. Luhtanen

SUMMARY. This study investigated and compared predictors of well-being in lesbians/bisexual women and gay/bisexual men. Well-being was assessed using measures of self-esteem, life satisfaction, and depression. Predictor variables included involvement in lesbian/gay/bisexual (LGB) culture, rejection of negative stereotypes of LGBs, positivity of gay/lesbian identity, and perceived acceptance by family, heterosexual friends, and work/school associates. A survey instrument was developed

Riia K. Luhtanen, PhD, is a research associate, Institute for Social Research, University of Michigan.

Address correspondence to: Riia K. Luhtanen, RCGD/Institute for Social Research, P.O. Box 1428, University of Michigan, Ann Arbor, MI 48106 (E-mail: riia@umich.edu).

The data reported here constitute a part of the author's dissertation project at the State University of New York at Buffalo where she received her degree in Social Psychology in 1995. Thanks are due to Jennifer Crocker (graduate advisor); Charles Behling, Barbara Bunker, Joel Raynor, and Wayne Bylsma (dissertation committee members); Dawn Green and David Quirolo (undergraduate assistants); the lesbian, gay and bisexual men and women who participated in this project; and the Mark Diamond Research Fund of the Graduate Student Association, State University of New York at Buffalo, which funded most of this research.

[Haworth co-indexing entry note]: "Identity, Stigma Management, and Well-Being: A Comparison of Lesbians/Bisexual Women and Gay/Bisexual Men." Luhtanen, Riia K. Co-published simultaneously in *Journal of Lesbian Studies* (Harrington Park Press, an imprint of The Haworth Press, Inc.) Vol. 7, No. 1, 2003, pp. 85-100; and: *Mental Health Issues for Sexual Minority Women: Redefining Women's Mental Health* (ed: Tonda L. Hughes, Carrol Smith, and Alice Dan) Harrington Park Press, an imprint of The Haworth Press, Inc., 2003, pp. 85-100. Single or multiple copies of this article are available for a fee from The Haworth Document Delivery Service [1-800-HAWORTH, 9:00 a.m. - 5:00 p.m. (EST). E-mail address: getinfo@haworthpressinc.com].

   85

and distributed in the Greater Buffalo area in Spring and Summer of 1994, to which 168 lesbians and bisexual women and 152 gay and bisexual men responded. Overall, results were very similar for lesbian/bisexual women and gay/bisexual men. Having a positive LGB identity was the most robust predictor of psychological well-being in both women and men who participated in the study. In addition, rejection of negative stereotypes predicted positive LGB identity. Results are discussed within the context of lesbian/bisexual women's mental health and suggestions for research and practice are described. *[Article copies available for a fee from The Haworth Document Delivery Service: 1-800-HAWORTH. E-mail address: <getinfo@haworthpressinc.com> Website: <http://www.HaworthPress.com> © 2003 by The Haworth Press, Inc. All rights reserved.]*

KEYWORDS. Lesbians, gay men, bisexuals, mental health, psychological well-being, depression, self-esteem

The experience of prejudice and discrimination by stigmatized individuals can have negative psychological consequences. For example, groups marginalized from the mainstream culture have been found to be at increased risk for depression (McGrath, Keita, Strickland, & Russo, 1990). Because of isolation and alienation from the predominately heterosexual culture, sexual minorities are believed to be particularly vulnerable to psychological distress (McColl, 1994; Stein, 1993). However, research on the psychological effects of stigma on people in general (Crocker & Major, 1989), and on lesbians and gay men in particular (Luhtanen, 1995), are mixed. Further, less research has focused on lesbians and bisexual women than on gay and bisexual men–perhaps because gay/bisexual men are more often the targets of antigay harassment and violence. However, lesbian/bisexual women may be at higher risk than gay/bisexual men for psychological distress because of their multiple minority status as women and as members of a sexual minority population (Cochran & Mays, 1994; DiPlacido, 1998).

This study examines some of the factors that have been theoretically or empirically linked to psychological distress in lesbians, gay men, or bisexual women and men (LGBs) such as self-disclosure of sexual identity (visibility), involvement with other LGBs, perceived acceptance by others of one's sexual orientation, rejection of negative stereotypes, and positivity of LGB identity. The relationships of these variables to psychological well-being in lesbians/bisexual women and gay/bisexual men are examined and compared.

LGB Visibility. Several models of lesbian and gay identity development propose a series of cognitive, behavioral and affective changes. These changes involve increasing acceptance of the label "homosexual"; movement from initial internalization or acceptance of negative stereotypes to rejection of them and development of a positive attitude toward homosexuality; use of various strategies to avoid the stigma associated with being LGB; increasingly more frequent affiliation with other LGB people and socialization into the LGB subculture; and greater disclosure of sexual identity to others (Cass, 1984; Cox & Gallois, 1996; Garnets & Kimmel, 1991; Marszalek & Cashwell, 1999; Troiden, 1989).

Most LGB identity theorists propose that self-disclosure of sexual identity is associated with psychological well-being, and that self-disclosure to all others is an indication of a completely integrated and positive LGB identity (Cass, 1979; Lee, 1977). In other words, these theorists seem to posit that full self-disclosure of one's sexual identity is a *consequence* of having a positive self-concept and high self-esteem. On the other hand, humanistic psychologists (e.g., Maslow, 1954) and others argue that self-disclosure brings about congruency between the real self and the public self and is an important precondition to (i.e., *cause* of) a healthy identity and self-esteem. Studies show that closeted LGBs tend to hold negative attitudes toward homosexuality and to score lower on measures of psychological well-being, and that self-disclosure is associated with positive LGB identity and psychological adjustment (McDonald, 1982; Miranda & Storms, 1989; Weinberg & Williams, 1974). However, in a review of studies examining these relationships, Savin-Williams (1990) concluded that although there appears to be a fairly consistent positive relationship between coming out to self (i.e., labeling and acceptance of oneself as LGB) and self-esteem, evidence for the relationship between disclosure to others and self-esteem is mixed. Although fewer studies of these relationships have focused on lesbians and bisexual women, greater sexual identity disclosure appears to be related to lower levels of psychological distress in women as well as men (Morris, Waldo, & Rothblum, 2001).

Involvement with Other LGBs. The LGB community provides acceptance, friendship, and potential romantic and sexual partners. It also "legitimizes" same-sex feelings and behavior, and offers validation in the form of helping LGBs interpret and understand their experiences and resist the societal assumptions that homosexuality or bisexuality is shameful and sick (Frable, Platt, & Hoey, 1998; Ponse, 1980; Weinberg & Williams, 1974). Perhaps the most robust empirical finding with regard to predicting self-esteem in studies of LGB samples is that social support in the form of affiliation with other LGBs is positively related to self-esteem and psychological well-being. Higher levels of self-esteem, better psychological adjustment (including less depression), and fewer personal problems in LGBs who are involved in the LGB subculture, compared to those who have little involvement, have been found in many studies (D'Augelli, Collins, & Hart, 1987; Jacobs & Tedford, 1980; Kurdek, 1988).

Perceived Acceptance. The beneficial effects of social support also appear to extend beyond the support of the LGB community (Goldfried & Goldfried, 2001; Grossman, D'Augelli, & Hershberger, 2000; Kurdek, 1988). For example, Savin-Williams (1990) found that self-esteem in gay male youth was related to perceived support from family and friends. LGB youth who experience acceptance are less likely to be depressed or suicidal than those who do not (Safren & Heimberg, 1999). Hammersmith and Weinberg (1973) found that social support in the form of acceptance of gay men's homosexuality by heterosexual significant others (e.g., family members, heterosexual friends, work associates) was associated with higher levels of self-esteem and other indicators of psychological adjustment. Similarly, Oetjen and Rothblum (2000) found that perceived social support from friends and family was negatively associated with depression in lesbians.

Rejection of Negative Stereotypes. Rejecting the idea that homosexuality or bisexuality is an illness or is immoral is important in the development of positive LGB identity and psychological adjustment (McDonald, 1982; Myer & Dean, 1998; Szymanski, Chung, & Balsam, 2001). Although previous research has found that endorsement of negative stereotypes is associated with lower self-esteem, this relationship may be mediated by how LGB individuals feel about their sexual identity. In other words, cognitively rejecting negative notions about LGBs in general is not likely a powerful predictor of well-being unless it is accompanied by positive feelings about one's own sexual orientation.

Positivity of LGB Identity. LGB positivity means that being lesbian, gay, or bisexual is perceived as valid, positive, natural and normal, and an "essential identity"–a state of being or a way of life rather than simply a behavior or particular sexual orientation (Troiden, 1989). For example, Frable, Wortman and Joseph (1997) found that positive gay identity was predictive of self-esteem, well-being and adjustment, but contact with other gays was not directly associated with positive self-perceptions. Rather, having gay friends and attending gay social events appeared to reinforce positive gay identity, which in turn predicted self-esteem, psychological well-being and adjustment. Similarly, Miranda and Storms (1989) found that self-labeling as lesbian/gay was related to satisfaction with lesbian/gay identity which in turn was associated with psychological adjustment. It is noteworthy that achieving a positive minority identity is not only important for LGBs: having a positive *ethnic* identity has also been shown to predict psychological well-being in ethnic minorities (Martinez & Dukes, 1997).

METHODS

Instrument and Measures

Data were collected for this study using an anonymous "Lesbian, Gay, and Bisexual Survey" that was distributed with self-addressed, postage-paid envelopes to lesbians, gay men and bisexual women and men in the greater Buffalo area. The survey instrument included questions about demographic and background characteristics, level of involvement in the LGB community, and perceptions of others' acceptance of the respondent's sexual orientation. In addition, several scales were included to assess psychological well-being and factors believed to predict psychological well-being.

Psychological Well-Being. Psychological well-being was operationally defined in this study using three measures: self-esteem, life-satisfaction, and depression. Self-esteem was assessed using the Rosenberg (1965) Self-Esteem Scale, a widely used and well-validated 10-item measure of global personal self-esteem (alpha = .91 for women; .88 for men). Life satisfaction was measured using the 5-item Satisfaction with Life Scale (SWLS; Diener, Emmons, Larsen, & Griffin, 1985). For both of these scales, responses ranged from 1 ("Strongly disagree") to 7 ("Strongly agree") and were averaged (alpha = .87 for women; .84 for men). Depression was assessed using the 20-item Center for Epidemiologic Studies Depression Scale (CES-D) (Radloff, 1977). Responses to questions about various symptoms were made on a scale from 1 (the symptom occurring "rarely or none of the time [less than 1 day]) to 4 (most or all of the time [5-7 days] during the past week). Scores were averaged with an overall scale score that ranged from 1 to 4. This method of scoring differs from the more usual scoring from 0 to 3, with total scores ranging from 0 to 60. Whereas with score ranges of 0 to 60 a score greater than 15 indicates probable clinical depression, using our method of scoring a score greater than 2.0 indicates probable clinical depression. Alphas for the CES-D were .92 for women and .93 for men in the study. The three measures of psychological well-being were highly correlated (r's ranged from .63 to .69).

Visibility was assessed using a scale adapted from Weinberg and Williams (1974) that asked the respondents "Of each of the following people, how many definitely know about your sexual orientation (in that you have actually told them or discussed it with them)?" Responses ranged from 1 (none) to 7 (all) with a midpoint of 4 (about half). Categories of people included (1) heterosexuals whom you know, (2) female heterosexual friends, (3) male heterosexual friends, (4) relatives, (5) neighbors, and (6) work associates/classmates. Average scores were calculated for each category of people (alphas = .91 for women; .88 for men).

Involvement in the LGB Culture. This variable was measured using responses to two questions: (1) "How many of your friends are gay/lesbian/bisexual?"; and (2) "What proportion of your leisure time do you spend with gays/lesbians/bisexuals?" Responses to each of these questions ranged from 1 (none) to 7 (all). Scores were averaged to create an index of involvement (alphas = .75 for women; .80 for men).

Perceived Acceptance was assessed by asking the respondents to indicate, on a scale from 1 ("extremely nonsupportive or rejecting") to 7 ("extremely supportive or accepting"), the extent to which the following individuals accepted and were supportive of the respondent's sexual orientation: mother (or female guardian), father (or male guardian), closest brother, closest sister, closest heterosexual male friend, closest heterosexual female friend, boss/supervisor at work, closest teacher at school, closest work associate, and closest classmate at school. Because some of these relationships were not applicable to all respondents, three indexes were created that reflected average scores for perceived acceptance by (1) family (mother, father, brother, sister); (2) heterosexual friends (male friend, female friend), and (3) work/school associates (boss/supervisor, teacher, work associate, classmate).

Rejection of Negative Stereotypes was measured using responses to the following five questions: "In general, heterosexuals tend to be more emotionally stable or better adjusted than gay men and lesbians"; "There is nothing immoral about homosexuality"; "Heterosexuality is more natural than homosexuality"; "Gay men and lesbians are just as capable of maintaining intimate relationships as are heterosexuals"; and "Lesbians and gay men are not as fit to be parents as are heterosexuals." Response scale was from 1 ("Strongly disagree") to 7 ("Strongly agree") for each of the questions; scores on negatively worded items were reversed and scores were then averaged to create an overall scale score (alphas = .61 for women; .59 for men).

Positivity of LGB Identity was assessed by the following four items: "I feel good about who I am in terms of my sexual orientation"; "I would not give up my sexual orientation even if I could"; "I often regret that I am who I am in terms of my sexual orientation"; and "If there were a magic pill that would make me straight, I would take it." As in the questions above, scale scores on negatively worded questions were reversed, and scores were then averaged to arrive at an overall score reflecting positivity of LGB identity (alphas = .80 for women; .79 for men).

Data Analysis

Data analysis was conducted in three phases. First, bivariate analyses were conducted to compare lesbian/bisexual women and gay/bisexual men with regard to the demographic characteristics and levels of the predictor and outcome variables. Second, partial correlation analyses were conducted to investigate the relationships between the predictor variables and the outcome (i.e., well-being) variables, comparing males and females. Third, regression analyses were used to determine which variables were the strongest predictors of well-being and of positive LGB identity.

Data Collection Procedure

Approximately 3000 copies of the survey questionnaire were distributed in the Greater Buffalo area during the spring and summer of 1994. A cover letter introduced the principal investigator, described the purpose of the study and its importance, and provided information about where to call with questions or concerns. Participants were assured that their responses would be anonymous. Two copies were mailed to the approximately 500 individuals on the Buffalo Gay, Lesbian, Bisexual, Transgender and Transsexual Community Network's mailing list. Recipients of these questionnaires were asked to complete one of the surveys themselves and to give the second one to an LGB friend. The remainder of the surveys were distributed in Buffalo's lesbian and gay bars, and through various local gay organizations. The majority of respondents (41%) received the questionnaire by mail; 23% got it from a friend; 11% from a bar; and 25% from some other place (most of these likely received the questionnaire at meetings of local organizations). Although returned surveys accounted for only 10% of the total distributed, it is impossible to calculate a response rate. For example, because a large number of surveys were distributed at bars, it is likely that many of these were discarded rather than returned. Although questionnaires were distributed to organizations and businesses that serve racially diverse clients, recruitment efforts did not specifically target LGBs of color.

RESULTS

Description of the Sample

Table 1 summarizes the demographic characteristics of the sample. Respondents included 168 (52.5%) women and 152 (47.5%) men. Ages of respondents ranged from 19 to 73 years, with a mean age of 38 for women and 36 for men. The majority of the respondents (92.5%) identified as lesbian or gay; 23 (7.2%) identified as bisexual (17 women and 7 men). The sample was predominately white (92%) and well-educated (most had a college or graduate de-

TABLE 1. Means and Standard Deviations for Demographic Variables by Gender

	Lesbian and Bisexual Women			Gay and Bisexual Men			
	M (range)	sd	n	M (range)	sd	n	p
Demographics							
Age	38.12	10.33	164	35.54	11.46	149	< .04
Education	5.63 (2-8)	1.58	168	5.34 (2-8)	1.62	152	ns
Income	3.23 (1-8)	1.53	165	3.32 (1-11)	2.24	152	ns
Location of Residence	1.14 (1-2)	.35	166	1.06 (1-2)	.24	152	< .02
Relationship Status	1.72 (1-2)	.45	163	1.42 (1-2)	.50	147	< .001

Note. Education ranged from less than high school (1) to PhD, MD, or equivalent (8); Income ranged from less than $10,000/yr (1) to $80,000 (8); Location was coded city or suburb (1) or rural or small town (2); Relationship status was involved in a same-sex relationship (1) or not involved (2).
p = significance level for comparisons of means by gender

gree). The average annual income was about $30,000. Most of the participants (89%) lived in a city or suburb. Slightly more than one-half (56%) were involved in a relationship with a same-sex partner. More women than men in the study identified as bisexual. In addition, the women were older on average, more likely to live in a small town or rural area, and more likely to be involved in a same-sex relationship. Because demographic characteristics and most of the study variables did not differ between bisexual women and lesbians or bisexual and gay men, and because the number of bisexual women and men was small, these groups were combined with lesbians and gay men.

Compared to Census estimates of Erie County (Bureau of the Census, 1998), the sample was more likely to be white (91% compared with 83% of the general population), have a college education (nearly 70% compared with 20%), and have higher average incomes (approximately $30,000 compared with $21,000).

Table 2 summarizes the mean scores of the two groups on each of the study variables. Lesbian/bisexual women did not differ from gay/bisexual men on any of the well-being variables. On average, both groups had high levels of self-esteem (similar to levels found in other studies of heterosexual and non-heterosexual samples), reasonable levels of life-satisfaction, and tended to score in the lower range on the CES-D. Overall, 55 (17%) of the respondents scored in the clinically depressed range (above 2.0). Interestingly, more men (24%) than women (14%) scored above 2 on the CES-D, though this difference was not statistically significant. Although women in the study were less

TABLE 2. Means, Standard Deviations, and Alphas for the Main Variables by Gender

	Lesbian/Bisexual Women			Gay/Bisexual Men			
	M (range)	sd	n	M (range)	sd	n	p
Predictor Variables							
Visibility	3.57 (1-7)	1.72	158	4.14 (1-7)	1.66	144	< .005
Involvement with other LGBs	4.74 (1-7)	1.23	168	4.75 (2-7)	1.21	151	ns
Family's Acceptance	5.11 (1-7)	1.57	148	5.08 (1-7)	1.61	134	ns
Heterosexual Friends' Acceptance	5.96 (1-7)	1.18	152	6.05 (1-7)	1.29	142	ns
Work/School Associates' Acceptance	5.73 (2-7)	1.22	152	5.52 (1-7)	1.47	125	ns
Rejection of Negative Stereotypes	6.44 (3-7)	.74	168	6.03 (3-7)	.92	152	< .001
Positive LGB Identity	6.24 (2-7)	1.04	168	5.83 (1-7)	1.34	151	< .004
Outcome Variables							
Self-Esteem	5.89 (2.7-7)	.91	168	5.79 (2-7)	1.03	152	ns
Life Satisfaction	4.78 (1-7)	1.42	168	4.68 (1-7)	1.38	152	ns
Depression	1.55 (1-3.4)	.51	166	1.59 (1-3.75)	.56	150	ns

p = significance level for gender comparisons

visible than their male counterparts ($p < .005$), they reported more positive LGB identity ($p < .005$) and were more likely to reject negative stereotypes of LGBs ($p < .001$). No other gender differences were found. Because income, education, location of residence, and involvement in a same-sex relationship were positively correlated with one or more of the well-being indicators, these variables, as well as respondents' age, were controlled for in subsequent analyses.

Table 3 presents the partial correlations between predictor variables and measures of well-being. Visibility, involvement with other LGBs, acceptance by family members, rejection of negative stereotypes, and positive LGB identity were all found to be positively correlated with the well-being indicators. The strength of the correlations were similar for women and men in the study.

TABLE 3. Partial Correlations Controlling for Age, Education, Income, Location, and Relationship Status

	Self-Esteem			Life Satisfaction			Depression		
	Women	Men	p	Women	Men	p	Women	Men	p
Visibility	.20**	.16*	ns	.21**	.12	ns	−.08	−.20**	ns
Involvement with Other LGBs	.15*	.22**	ns	.34***	.23**	ns	−.18*	−.16*	ns
Family's Acceptance	.16*	.26**	ns	.25**	.16*	ns	−.18*	−.24**	ns
Heterosexual Friends' Acceptance	.13	.37***	< .02	.15*	.25**	ns	−.12	−.30***	< .07
Work/School Associates' Acceptance	.02	.28**	< .03	.05	.21*	ns	.03	−.20**	< .04
Rejection of Negative Stereotypes	.28***	.31***	ns	.28***	.25**	ns	−.22**	−.29***	ns
Positivity of LGB Identity	.49***	.48***	ns	.45***	.42***	ns	−.37***	−.48***	ns

Note: N's vary because of missing data.
p = significance level for gender comparisons: *p < .05; **p < .01; ***p < .001

Perceived acceptance from heterosexual friends and acceptance from work or school associates, however, were more highly correlated with self-esteem (positively) and depression (negatively) for men, than for women. Although visibility was associated with well-being in both women and men, and women were as likely as men to be out to family members, they were less likely to be out to the other groups of people assessed in the study.

Given Frable et al.'s (1997) findings that having a positive sexual identity mediated the effect of visibility on positive self-perception in gay men, a series of partial correlations were run controlling for positivity of LGB identity and the demographic characteristics described above. In these analyses the relationships between visibility and the well-being indicators were not significant for either men or women in the study (see Table 4). For men, heterosexual friends' acceptance was significantly associated with each of the well-being indicators, family acceptance was significantly correlated with self-esteem and depression, and work/school associate acceptance was positively correlated with self-esteem. For women in the study, only the association between family acceptance and life satisfaction was significant. Thus, it appears that

TABLE 4. Partial Correlations Controlling for Age, Education, Income, Location, Relationship Status and Positivity of LGB Identity

	Self-Esteem		Life Satisfaction		Depression	
	Women	Men	Women	Men	Women	Men
Visibility	.10	.06	.12	.03	−.01	−.11
Family's Acceptance	.06	.21*	.17*	.10	−.11	−.19*
Heterosexual Friends' Acceptance	.06	.28***	.08	.15*	−.06	−.20**
Work/School Associates' Acceptance	−.08	.19*	−.03	.11	.11	−.09

Note: N's vary because of missing data. Mean visibility of females vs. males, respectively, to the specific target groups were as follows: relatives 3.55 vs. 3.65 (ns); heterosexuals whom one knows 3.71 vs. 4.45 ($p < .001$); heterosexual female friends 4.45 vs. 4.87 ($p < .09$); heterosexual male friends 3.76 vs. 4.39 ($p < .02$); neighbors 2.40 vs. 3.43 ($p < .001$); and work associates/classmates 3.39 vs. 4.0 ($p < .02$).
*$p < .05$; **$p < .01$; ***$p < .001$

lesbians and bisexual women are less open about their sexual orientation and may consider it less important to come out to people other than family members, even though they report levels of perceived acceptance comparable to those of their male counterparts. Psychological well-being appears less associated with others' acceptance among lesbian and bisexual women, than gay and bisexual men, in this study.

Next, separate multiple regression analyses for women and men in the study were conducted to determine the relative power of the independent variables in predicting each of the three indicators of psychological well-being. These analyses included all the predictor variables and controlled for age, education, income, location of residence, and relationship status. The first analyses examined regression models predicting self-esteem. For women, only positive LGB identity was a significant predictor of self-esteem scores (Beta = .42; t = 3.85; $p = .001$). The variables as a whole explained 29% of the variance in women's self-esteem. Similarly, only positive LGB identity predicted self-esteem scores among men in the sample (Beta = .31; t = 2.90; $p = .006$); the overall model accounted for 41% of the variance in men's self-esteem scores.

Second, the same variables were used to test predictive models of life satisfaction. Two variables were significant predictors of life satisfaction for women: involvement with other LGBs (Beta = .20; t = 2.18; $p = .04$) and positive identity (Beta = .33, t = 2.98; $p = .005$). The overall model accounted for 29% of the variance in women's life satisfaction scores. Only positive LGB identity significantly predicted life satisfaction for men (Beta = .25; t = 2.18; p = .04); the model accounted for 31% of the variance in life satisfaction scores for men.

Third, regression analyses were used to predict depression scores of the respondents. Only two variables were significant predictors of level of depression among women: rejection of negative stereotypes (Beta = −.26; t = −2.10; p = .04) and positive LGB identity (Beta = −26; t = −2.30; p = .03). The overall model accounted for 25% of the variance in depression scores for lesbian/bisexual women. The only significant predictor of depression for gay/bisexual men was positive LGB identity (Beta = −.36; t = −3.61; p = .001).

Finally, given that positive LGB identity was such a strong predictor of psychological well-being, two additional regression models were tested using positive LGB identity as the dependent variable. The only significant predictor of positive identity for women was rejection of negative stereotypes (Beta = .50; t = 5.25; p = .001). The model accounted for 37% of the variance in women's LGB identity scores. For gay and bisexual men, rejection of negative stereotypes (Beta = .49; t = 5.60; p = .001) and acceptance by heterosexual friends (Beta = .32; t = 3.0; p = .004) were significant predictors of positive LGB identity. The overall model accounted for 43% of the variance in LGB identity scores.

DISCUSSION

Overall, results of this study were similar for women and men. Partial correlations indicate that visibility, rejection of negative stereotypes, acceptance from family, involvement with other LGBs, and positivity of LGB identity were all significantly related to higher self-esteem and life satisfaction, and lower depression scores in both women and men. This finding is similar to those of earlier studies of mostly gay men (McDonald, 1982; Kurdek, 1988). For both women and men in the study, having a positive LGB identity was the most robust predictor of psychological well-being. In addition, rejection of negative stereotypes predicted positive LGB identity for both women and men–thus reinforcing the importance of rejecting negative stereotypes of LGBs to the development of a positive sexual identity and in fostering the psychological well-being of lesbians, gay men, and bisexual women and men.

Interestingly, findings from the partial correlations suggest that social support in the form of acceptance by heterosexual friends and work/school associates are significantly associated with higher levels of self-esteem and lower scores on the depression measure in gay/bisexual men but not in lesbian/bisexual women. This is counter to findings by Oetjen and Rothblum (2000), which indicated that perceived social support from friends was a potent negative predictor of depression among lesbians and bisexual women. One possible explanation of this difference is that in the present study, respondents were asked about perceived acceptance from *heterosexual* friends, whereas Oetjen and Rothblum assessed perceived support from friends in general. Considering that lesbian/bisexual women in the current study were less visible or out to others (except for family members) than were gay/bisexual men, acceptance from other individuals may be less salient to women in the study. It is possible that acceptance from close LGB friends (not assessed here) would have been a stronger predictor of psychological well-being among women in the study.

Limitations of this study include the use of a convenience sample and the low response rate. In addition, the sample was very homogeneous and consisted of mostly white, well-educated adults, who lived in a limited geographical area. Also, the participants were quite well off both psychologically and financially, well connected to the LGB community, and relatively open regarding their sexual identity. Finally, there were too few bisexual women and men to permit separate analyses by gender and sexual orientation. Although demographically similar to lesbians and gay men in the study, it is possible bisexual women and men may differ from their lesbian and gay counterparts on some of the variables included in the study. For example, bisexual women and men may be less visible and less involved in the LGB culture. These factors may serve to reduce the risk of discrimination and harassment, but may limit social support. In the future, researchers should make a concerted effort to recruit large enough numbers of these groups to permit valid comparisons. Clearly, this sample is not representative of all LGB people–especially bisexual women and men and LGB people of color. Homogeneous samples are a common limitation of LGB studies because it is hard to recruit participants who are uncomfortable disclosing their sexual identity and therefore not likely to be connected to gay groups and organizations where samples can be accessed most economically. Studies of sexual minority women's (and men's) mental health that have greater representation of racial/ethnic minorities are needed. Such representation is essential to determine whether psychological risk factors differ among racial/ethnic sexual minority groups. For example, conflicts between multiple minority identities may lead to increased risk for isolation from both the cultural group and from predominantly white LGB communities and organizations (Cabaj & Stein, 1996).

In summary, although findings cannot be generalized to other groups of LGB women and men, they suggest directions for future research and practice. For example, it appears that an important predictor of psychological well-being, regardless of gender, is having a positive sexual identity and that rejection of negative stereotypes is important to developing a positive sexual identity.

Although discrimination against LGBs is still widespread, the lessening stigma associated with same-sex relationships may serve to foster more positive identities among sexual minority women and men. However, until laws protecting the civil rights of LGB persons are widespread and uniformly enforced, concerted efforts by mental health and other health care professionals are needed to assist LGB youth and adults to develop positive sexual identities.

REFERENCES

The Bureau of the Census (1998). Estimates of the population of counties by age, sex and race/Hispanic origin: 1990 to 1997. Available: *http://govinfo.library.orst.edu/* [17 Aug. 2001].

Cabaj, R.P., & Stein, T.S. (Eds.) (1996). *Textbook of homosexuality and mental health.* Washington, DC: American Psychiatric Press.

Cass, V.C. (1979). Homosexual identity formation: A theoretical model. *Journal of Homosexuality, 4,* 219-235.

Cass, V.C. (1984). Homosexual identity formation: Testing a theoretical model. *Journal of Sex Research, 20,* 143-167.

Cochran, S.D., & Mays, V.M. (1994). Depressive distress among homosexually active African American men and women. *American Journal of Psychiatry, 151*(4), 524-529.

Cox, S., & Gallois, C. (1996). Gay and lesbian identity development: A social identity. *Journal of Homosexuality, 30,* 1-30.

Crocker, J., & Major, B. (1989). Social stigma and self-esteem: The self-protective properties of stigma. *Psychological Review, 96,* 608-630.

D'Augelli, A.R., Collins, C., & Hart, M.M. (1987). Social support patterns of lesbian women in a rural helping network. *Journal of Rural Community Psychology, 8,* 12-21.

Diener, E., Emmons, A., Larsen, R.J., & Griffin, S. (1985). The Satisfaction with Life Scale: A measure of life satisfaction. *Journal of Personality Assessment, 49,* 71-75.

DiPlacido, J. (1998). Minority stress among lesbians, gay men, and bisexuals: A consequence of heterosexism, homophobia, and stigmatization. In G.M. Herek (Ed.), *Stigma and sexual orientation: Understanding prejudice against lesbians, gay men, and bisexuals* (pp. 138-159) Thousand Oaks, CA: Sage Publications.

Frable, D., Wortman, C., & Joseph, J. (1997). Predicting self-esteem, well-being, and distress in a cohort of gay men: The importance of cultural stigma, personal visibility, community networks, and positive identity. *Journal of Personality, 65,* 599-624.

Frable, D., Platt, L., & Hoey, S. (1998). Concealable stigmas and positive self-perceptions: Feeling better around similar others. *Journal of Personality and Social Psychology, 74,* 909-922.

Garnets, L., & Kimmel, D. (1991). Lesbian and gay male dimensions in the psychological study of human diversity. In J. Goodchilds (Ed.), *Psychological perspectives on human diversity in America.* Washington, DC: American Psychological Association.

Goldfried, M.R., & Goldfried, A.P. (2001). The importance of parental support in the lives of gay, lesbian, and bisexual individuals. *Journal of Clinical Psychology, 57,* 681-693.

Grossman, A.H., D'Augelli, A.R., & Hershberger, S.L. (2000). Social support networks of lesbian, gay, and bisexual adults 60 years of age and older. *Journal of Gerontology, 55B*, 171-179.

Hammersmith, S.K., & Weinberg, M.S. (1973). Homosexual identity: Commitment, adjustment and significant others. *Sociometry, 36*, 56-79.

Jacobs, J.A., & Tedford, W.H. (1980). Factors affecting self-esteem of the homosexual individual. *Journal of Homosexuality, 5*, 373-382.

Kurdek, L.A. (1988). Perceived social support in gays and lesbians in cohabiting relationships. *Journal of Personality and Social Psychology, 54*, 504-509.

Lee, J.A. (1977). Going public: A study in the sociology of homosexual liberation. *Journal of Homosexuality, 3*, 49-77.

Luhtanen, R. (1996). Identity, stigma management and psychological well-being in lesbians and gay men. *Dissertation Abstracts International: Section B: The Sciences and Engineering, 56*, 10B. (UMI No. 9603624)

Marszalek, J.F., & Cashwell, C.S. (1999). The gay and lesbian affirmative development (GLAD) model: Applying Ivey's developmental counseling therapy model to Cass' gay and lesbian identity development model. *Adultspan Journal, 1*, 13-31.

Martinez, R.O., & Dukes, R.L. (1997). The effects of ethnic identity, ethnicity, and gender on adolescent well-being. *Journal of Youth and Adolescence, 26*, 503-516.

Maslow, A.H. (1954). *Motivation and personality*. New York: Harper.

McColl, P. (1994). Homosexuality and mental health services. *British Medical Journal, 308*, 550-551.

McDonald, G.J. (1982). Individual differences in the coming out process for gay men: Implications for theoretical models. *Journal of Homosexuality, 8*, 47-60.

McGrath, E., Keita, G.P., Strickland, B.R., & Russo, N.F. (Eds.) (1990). *Women and depression: Risk factors and treatment issues*. Washington, DC: American Psychological Association.

Miranda, J., & Storms, M. (1989). Psychological adjustment of lesbians and gay men. *Journal of Counseling and Development, 68*, 41-45.

Morris, J.F., Waldo, C.R., & Rothblum, E.D. (2001). A model of predictors and outcomes of outness among lesbian and bisexual women. *American Journal of Orthopsychiatry, 71*, 61-71.

Myer, I.H., & Dean, L. (1998). Internalized homophobia, intimacy, and sexual behavior among gay and bisexual men. In G. Herek (Ed.), *Stigma and sexual orientation: Understanding prejudice against lesbians, gay men, and bisexuals* (pp. 160-186). Thousand Oaks, CA: Sage.

Oetjen, H., & Rothblum, E.D. (2000). When lesbians aren't gay: Factors affecting depression among lesbians. *Journal of Homosexuality, 39*, 49-73.

Ponse, B. (1980). Lesbians and their worlds. In J. Marmor (Ed.), *Homosexual behavior: A modern reappraisal* (pp. 157-175). New York: Basic Books.

Radloff, L.S. (1977). The CES-D Scale: A self-report depression scale for research in the general population. *Applied Psychological Measurement, 1*, 385-401.

Rosenberg, M. (1965). *Society and the adolescent self-image*. Princeton, NJ: Princeton University Press.

Safren, S.A., & Heimberg, R.G. (1999). Depression, hopelessness, suicidality, and related factors in sexual minority and heterosexual adolescents. *Journal of Consulting and Clinical Psychology, 67,* 859-866.

Savin-Williams, R.C. (1990). *Gay and lesbian youth: Expressions of identity.* New York: Hemisphere Publishing Co.

Stein, T.S. (1993). Overview of new developments in understanding homosexuality. In J.M. Oldham, M.B. Riba, & A. Tasman (Eds.), *Review of Psychiatry, 12.* Washington, DC: American Psychiatric Press.

Szymanski, D.M., Chung, Y.B., & Balsam, K.F. (2001). Psychosocial correlates of internalized homophobia in lesbians. *Measurement and Evaluation in Counseling and Development, 34,* 27-38.

Troiden, R.R. (1989). The formation of homosexual identities. *Journal of Homosexuality, 17,* 43-73.

Weinberg, M.S., & Williams, C.J. (1974). *Male homosexuals: Their problems and adaptations.* New York: Oxford University Press.

A Comparative Study
of Lesbian and Heterosexual Women
in Committed Relationships

Alicia K. Matthews
Jessica Tartaro
Tonda L. Hughes

SUMMARY. Data from a diverse sample of lesbians and a demographically matched group of heterosexual women were used to examine and compare lesbians' and heterosexual women's relationships. Findings suggest similarities in the broad relationship experiences of women in the sample including the importance of being in a committed relationship, shared values with partners on relationship issues, and division of labor. Contrary to previous research findings, lesbian and heterosexual women did not differ on overall frequency of sexual activity. Although

Alicia K. Matthews, PhD, is affiliated with the Department of Psychiatry, University of Chicago.

Jessica Tartaro, BS, is affiliated with the Department of Psychology, Arizona State University, Tempe, AZ.

Tonda L. Hughes, RN, PhD, FAAN, is affiliated with the Department of Public Health, Mental Health and Administrative Nursing, University of Illinois at Chicago.

Address correspondence to: Alicia K. Matthews, PhD, University of Chicago, Department of Psychiatry, 5841 S. Maryland Avenue (MC 3077), Chicago, IL 60637 (E-mail: Amatthew@yoda.bsd.uchicago.edu).

[Haworth co-indexing entry note]: "A Comparative Study of Lesbian and Heterosexual Women in Committed Relationships." Matthews, Alicia K., Jessica Tartaro, and Tonda L. Hughes. Co-published simultaneously in *Journal of Lesbian Studies* (Harrington Park Press, an imprint of The Haworth Press, Inc.) Vol. 7, No. 1, 2003, pp. 101-114; and: *Mental Health Issues for Sexual Minority Women: Redefining Women's Mental Health* (ed: Tonda L. Hughes, Carrol Smith, and Alice Dan) Harrington Park Press, an imprint of The Haworth Press, Inc., 2003, pp. 101-114. Single or multiple copies of this article are available for a fee from The Haworth Document Delivery Service [1-800-HAWORTH, 9:00 a.m. - 5:00 p.m. (EST). E-mail address: getinfo@haworthpressinc.com].

101

relationship violence was uncommon among participants in this study, indicators of poor conflict resolution strategies were moderately high in both lesbian and heterosexual couples. Use of mental health services for relationship problems was low and did not differ by sexual orientation. Understanding relationship dynamics in general, and in lesbian couples in particular, is important in the provision of appropriate and effective mental health resources and services. *[Article copies available for a fee from The Haworth Document Delivery Service: 1-800-HAWORTH. E-mail address: <getinfo@haworthpressinc.com> Website: <http://www.HaworthPress.com> © 2003 by The Haworth Press, Inc. All rights reserved.]*

KEYWORDS. Intimate relationships, relationship satisfaction, mental health, lesbians, heterosexual women

Until recently, studies on intimate relationships focused exclusively on heterosexual couples (e.g., Gottman & Krakoff, 1989; Markman, Floyd, Stanley, & Storaasli, 1988). In the past decade, however, researchers have begun to include lesbians in these studies (e.g., Blumstein & Schwartz, 1990; Klinkenberg & Rose, 1994; Greene & Boyd-Franklin, 1996; Peplau & Spaulding, 2000). Much of the early information about lesbians' relationships was written by mental health clinicians and thus tended to focus on clinical issues such as low sexual desire (e.g., Nichols, 1988).

At least two research studies support clinical reports of lower sexual activity or desire among lesbian couples. For example, in an in-depth study of couple relationships Blumstein and Schwartz (1983) compared heterosexual married, heterosexual unmarried, gay male, and lesbian couples and found that of the four groups, lesbian couples reported the lowest rates of genital sexual activity. Similarly, Laumann and colleagues (1994) also found low frequency of genital sexual activity among lesbian respondents in their large population-based study on adult sexual activity. Some authors have posited that female socialization and an underdeveloped sex drive in women may account for lower sexual activity reported by lesbians (Nichols, 1988; Schreiner-Engel, 1986). On the other hand, Kotulski (1996) suggests that lesbian couples may be more likely than heterosexual couples to prefer non-genital expressions of sexuality and non-physical expressions of affection.

Studies comparing satisfaction in lesbian, gay male, and heterosexual couples raise interesting questions about the influence of gender and gender-roles on relationships (Blumstein & Schwartz, 1983; Kurdek & Schmitt, 1986; Haas & Stafford, 1998). For example, Green, Bettinger, and Zacks (1996) conducted a study of lesbian and gay male couples and compared findings with those from a large national study of heterosexual couples. Results suggested that lesbian and gay male couples showed greater equality and gender-role flexibility than heterosexual couples (Green et al., 1996). In two other studies, lesbian couples were more cohesive and reported higher satisfaction than either gay male or heterosexual couples (Kurdek, 1988; Zacks, Green, & Morrow, 1988).

Predictors of relationship satisfaction in lesbian couples appear similar to those in heterosexual couples. For example, in a study of 275 lesbian couples, Eldridge and Gilbert (1990) found that relationship satisfaction was positively associated with dyadic attachment, balance of power, intimacy, self-esteem, and life satisfaction. Also consistent with patterns found in heterosexual couples, this study found that relationship satisfaction was inversely associated with role conflict and drive toward personal autonomy.

Relationship violence in same-sex couples has received scant attention in the literature (Farley, 1996; Marrujo & Kreger, 1996). Recent studies exploring domestic violence in lesbian samples suggest that 22% to 46% of lesbians have experienced physical violence in their relationships with women (Elliot, 1996), rates comparable with those found among women in the general population. As in heterosexual couples, risk factors for domestic violence in same-sex relationships include power or status disparities (Goglucci, 2000; Stark & Flitcraft, 1988), dependence (Renzetti, 1988, 1992), isolation (Morrow & Hawxhurst, 1989; Waldner-Haugrud, Vaden Gratch, & Magruder, 1997), unemployment (Goglucci, 2000), alcohol abuse (Farley, 1996; Schilit, Lie, & Morrow, 1990), past experiences of abuse (Farley, 1996), and stress (Seltzer & Kalmuss, 1988). However, issues related to partner violence in lesbian and gay relationships are even more complex than those in heterosexual relationships. In addition to risk factors found in heterosexual violent relationships, internalized homophobia and fear of sexual orientation disclosure also appear to play an important role in domestic violence among same-sex couples (Elliot, 1996). The threat of disclosing a partner's sexual orientation to family members, employers, or others is a unique form of control in some same-sex couples. Very few resources exist for the victim or the perpetrator of violence in same-sex relationships. Further, the isolation associated with being a member of a stigmatized and marginalized population, and the societal tendency to blame the victims of violence, make it exceedingly difficult for lesbians and gay men to seek help.

Although the studies reviewed above provide important information about same-sex relationships, much more research is needed to better understand similarities and differences between lesbian and heterosexual women in committed relationships. This study examines a number of theoretically relevant variables using a diverse sample of lesbians and heterosexual women who are in committed relationships.

METHODS

Sampling and Recruitment of Survey Participants

Data for this project were collected as part of a larger study–the Chicago Health and Life Experiences of Women Study (CHLEW). This study was conducted in 1996 and 1997 to explore risk and protective factors for heavy drinking and drinking-related problems among lesbians. Women who self-identified as lesbian, were English speaking, and were 18 years old or older were recruited using a broad range of sources in Chicago and the surrounding suburbs. For example, advertisements were placed in local newspapers; flyers were posted in churches and bookstores, and distributed to formal organizations and via formal and informal social events and social networks. To increase the diversity of the study sample, racial/ethnic minority and other hard-to-reach women (e.g., older lesbians and those with lower incomes) were specifically targeted in advertisements and outreach efforts.

The heterosexual comparison group was obtained by asking each lesbian participant to help recruit a heterosexual woman of the same race and who had a job or role (including student, homemaker, or retiree) as similar as possible to the lesbians' own. Despite earlier success in having lesbian participants assist in recruitment of the heterosexual comparison group (Hughes, Haas, & Avery, 1997; Hughes, Haas, Razzano, Cassidy, & Matthews, 2000), the method did not work as well in this study. Possible reasons include lack of anonymity, time required to complete the interview (approximately 60-90 minutes), lower salience of the research topic to heterosexual women, and sensitivity of many of the questions. Offering a $10 incentive to lesbians for their assistance was only partially successful. Advertisements and social network referrals were used to find heterosexual matches for about one-third of the lesbian sample. Nevertheless, the final sample included 63 self-identified lesbians and a comparison group of 57 heterosexual women who were demographically very similar to the lesbian group. Of those, 36 lesbians and 33 heterosexual women were in a committed relationship at the time of the interview (e.g., married, in a committed relationship and living with a partner, or in a committed relationship but not living with a partner) and formed the basis of the analyses presented here.

Interview Procedures

Interested women were asked to call the project office to schedule an interview at a time and location convenient to them. Four trained female interviewers from diverse racial/ethnic backgrounds conducted the survey interviews; an attempt was made to match the race/ethnicity of the interviewer with that of the study participant. The majority of the questionnaire was administered face-to-face. Confidential self-administered handouts were used to collect data on sensitive topics, such as sexual experiences. Interviews were usually conducted in respondents' homes and lasted 60 to 90 minutes. Respondents received $20 for their time.

Measures

Interviewers administered a slightly modified version of the National Study of Health and Life Experiences of Women Study Questionnaire (R. Wilsnack, S. Wilsnack, & Klassen, 1984; S. Wilsnack, Klassen, Shur, & R. Wilsnack, 1991), adapted to make questions more inclusive of lesbians' experiences (Skrockie, 1996). Other modifications included more extensive questions about smoking and mental health services use. The Health and Life Experiences of Women questionnaire (HLEW) is used in an ongoing longitudinal study of women's drinking (see Hughes, Johnson, & S. Wilsnack, 2001, for a more detailed description of the instrument). The HLEW includes approximately 400 questions covering a variety of health concerns of women. Following is a description of the measures used in our analyses.

Sexual orientation. Women who identified as either lesbian or heterosexual were the target sample for the study. Although the study instrument included multiple measures of sexual orientation (i.e., those addressing identity, behavior, and attraction), self-identity was used to determine both sexual orientation and eligibility for the study. Women were screened for eligibility and were enrolled into the study if they described their sexual identity as lesbian/gay/homosexual or heterosexual. Women who identified as bisexual were excluded.

Relationship Issues and Satisfaction

Congruency of values. Respondents were asked how often they agreed with their partners on religious matters, demonstration of affection, major decisions, career decisions, and sexual relations. Responses ranged from 0 = "always disagree" to 5 = "always agree."

Division of labor. To explore the degree of equity in the distribution of household and other tasks, respondents were asked how often their partner takes responsibility for child care, major repairs, cooking, cleaning and other household chores, and earning income outside the home. Responses were on a 5-point scale ranging from 0 = "never" to 4 = "always."

Frequency and satisfaction with sex. Respondents were asked how frequently they have sexual activity with their partner (0 = "none" to 5 = "more than 3 times weekly"); how they usually feel about sexual activity with this partner (0 = "prefer it didn't happen" to 3 = "very good"); whether they want sex more often than their partner; and whether their partner wants sex more often than they. Responses to the last two questions were dichotomous (yes/no).

Relationship satisfaction. Respondents were asked how often they and their partner quarrel, get on each other's nerves, consider separating or terminating the relationship, and feel regret about becoming involved in the relationship. Responses were 0 = "never" to 5 = "all the time." In addition, respondents were asked how important it is to them to be married or in a committed relationship (0 = "not at all" to 5 = "very important").

Conflict resolution. To assess conflict resolution strategies, respondents were asked, "Has your current partner ever" (1) "insulted or sworn at you?" (2) "Sulked or refused to talk about a problem?" (3) "Stomped out of the house?" or (4) "Did or said something to spite you?" Responses to each question were dichotomous (0 = no, 1 = yes).

Relationship violence. Relationship violence was measured by asking women whether their partners had ever thrown something at them, pushed or hit them, or threatened to kill them with a weapon or in some other way (yes/no).

Use of mental health services. Respondents were asked whether they had sought help for relationship problems in the past five years (yes/no).

DATA ANALYSES

Data analyses included frequency distributions and calculations of descriptive statistics for relevant variables. Calculation of percentages, cross-tabulations, and chi square analyses were conducted to examine similarities and differences between lesbian and heterosexual women. Independent groups t-tests were conducted for continuous variables. All significant differences reported here have probabilities of $p < .05$.

RESULTS

Description of the sample. Table 1 presents the demographic characteristics of the 69 respondents (36 lesbian and 33 heterosexual) who were in a committed relationship at the time they were interviewed. The average age of participants was 39 years. The majority of women in the sample (65%) lived with their partners (19% were married)–34% did not live with their partner. Unlike the majority of lesbian health study samples that are predominately white, only 28% of this sample was white. The majority of women in the study had more

TABLE 1. Demographic Characteristics of Heterosexual and Lesbian Samples

	Heterosexual Women (N = 33)	Lesbians (N = 36)
	N (%)	N (%)
Average Age = 38.8 (range = 19-69)	38.75	38.97
Race/Ethnicity		
African American	10 (33)	15 (42)
Caucasian	9 (27)	10 (28)
Hispanic	8 (24)	10 (28)
Other	6 (18)	1 (03)
Education		
HS or less	3 (09)	6 (17)
Some college or BA/BS	18 (55)	19 (53)
Advanced Degree	12 (36)	11 (31)
Employment		
Full-time	22 (67)	19 (53)
Part-time	7 (21)	7 (19)
Other	4 (12)	10 (28)
Annual Income		
Less than $10,000	5 (15)	6 (17)
$10,000-49,999	18 (54)	18 (50)
$50,000 or more	10 (30)	12 (33)
Relationship Status		
Married	11 (33)	2 (06)*
Living with partner	12 (36)	20 (56)
Not living with partner	10 (30)	14 (38)

*p = .01

than a high school education (97%) and worked either full- or part-time (80%). The median household income was $30,000-$39,000. No significant differences were found between the lesbian and heterosexual groups on any of the demographic variables, except that more heterosexual women were married.

Congruency of values. Overall, both lesbians and heterosexual women reported that they and their partners agreed about life and relationship issues including religious matters (73%, 58%), demonstration of affection (59%, 58%), decision-making (68%, 61%), sexual relations (76%, 70%), and career decisions (79%, 64%).

Division of labor. Lesbians were more likely than heterosexual women to indicate that their partners "always" share in household tasks (27%, 12%) ($\chi^2 (4) = 10.5$, p ≤ .05). Differences between lesbians and heterosexual women on responsibility for earning income outside of the home (73%, 79%), cooking (36%, 42%) or cleaning (39%, 36%) were not statistically significant.

Lesbians were more likely to report that they "always" assume responsibility for major repairs (28%, 15%) (χ^2 (4) = 13.5, p ≤ .01).

Frequency and satisfaction with sexual activity. Lesbians were more likely than heterosexual women to report having had more than one sexual partner in the past 12 months (32%, 7%) (χ^2 (3) = 6.2, p ≤ .05). Similar proportions of lesbians (71%) and heterosexual women (68%) reported feeling "very good" about sex with their current sexual partner. Higher proportions of lesbians than heterosexual women reported that sex had been very important (62%, 48%) during their lifetime and more lesbians said that they frequently reach sexual climax during sexual activity (79%, 65%), though neither of these differences was statistically significant.

Frequency of current sexual activity was also similar for lesbians and heterosexual women. Sixty-nine percent of lesbians and 76% of heterosexual women reported having sex at least once per week. Only 30% of lesbians, compared with 70% of heterosexual women, reported that their partner wanted sex more often than they did (χ^2 (1) = 12.0, p ≤ .01). In contrast, 35% of lesbians compared with 7% of heterosexual women reported wanting sex more often than their partners (χ^2 (1) = 8.1, p ≤ .05).

Relationship satisfaction. Sixty-four percent of both lesbians and heterosexual women indicated that being married or in a committed relationship was important to them. However, although differences were not statistically significant, higher proportions of heterosexual women reported considering divorce (15%, 6%); frequent quarreling (24%, 15%); feeling regret about the relationship (6%, 3%); and "getting on each other's nerves" (24%, 12%). Heterosexual women (15%) were more likely than lesbians (0%) to report that they would like their partner to be different in "many ways" (χ^2 (3) = 8.24, p ≤ .05).

Conflict resolution. The majority of both lesbians (74%) and heterosexual women (70%) reported that it was easy to talk with their partners about a problem. However, more than one half of lesbians (58%) and heterosexual women (52%) reported that their partners had insulted or sworn at them during an argument. Higher (but not statistically significant) proportions of heterosexual women than lesbians reported that their partners had used the following conflict resolution strategies in the past year: sulking or refusing to talk about a problem (70%, 61%); stomping away during an argument (58%, 39%); and being spiteful (61%, 36%).

Relationship violence. Overall, 15% of the combined sample reported experiencing relationship violence. Thirteen percent of lesbians and 18% of heterosexual women reported that their current partner had ever thrown something at them, pushed them, or hit them. Only one participant–a heterosexual woman–reported having had a partner who threatened to kill her.

Use of mental health services. The majority of lesbians in the study (63%) had sought counseling or therapy in the past five years, a rate significantly higher than that reported by heterosexual women (39%) ($\chi^2(1)$ = 10.43, p ≤ .001). However, the percentages of lesbians (40%) and heterosexual women (46%) who reported use of mental health services for relationship problems did not differ.

DISCUSSION

Consistent with previous studies, we found many similarities in lesbians' and heterosexual women's reports of their relationships. The two groups had similar views about the importance of being in a committed relationship; shared life values and attitudes with their partners to similar degrees; and, with the exception of overall participation in household activities, reported a fairly equitable division of labor within their relationships.

The limited studies on balance of power within relationships have suggested similarities between lesbian and heterosexual couples (Chafetz, 1974; Kelly, 1972). In our study, similar proportions of lesbians and heterosexual women were responsible for earning income outside of the home indicating comparable economic power. However, earning one's own income is only one of several potential factors that might contribute to power imbalance in relationships. In a study conducted by Caldwell and Peplau (1984) imbalances of power were observed in 40% of the lesbian couples, although 97% of lesbians in the study valued equal power distribution. Disparities resulted from partners' unequal involvement in the relationship and level of personal resources, including education and income. Power imbalance was predictive of lower levels of relationship satisfaction in lesbians, whereas only heterosexual couples that reported a female-dominant style were dissatisfied with their relationship (Caldwell & Peplau, 1984). Additional studies are needed to clarify the factors that contribute to unequal power in lesbian couples and the impact of these factors on relationship satisfaction.

In contrast to previous findings suggesting lower frequency of sexual activity in lesbian couples (e.g., Blumstein & Schwartz, 1983), lesbians and heterosexual women in this sample did not differ on overall frequency of sexual activity. Further, lesbians and heterosexual women were equally likely to report that sexual activity had been very important during their lifetime, positive feelings about sexual activity with their partners, and that they almost always reached climax during sexual activity. However, an interesting pattern emerged regarding sexual desire. Heterosexual women were more likely than lesbians to report that their partners wanted sex more often than they. In contrast, lesbian respondents were more likely to report that they wanted sex more often than their partners. Although we did not explore the association between discrepant sexual desire and relationship satisfaction, earlier studies (e.g., Blumstein & Schwartz, 1983) suggest that this is an important topic for future research.

Overall, relationship violence was uncommon in our sample. However, indicators of poor conflict resolution strategies were moderately high across both lesbian and heterosexual couples. Studies with heterosexual populations have established a clear association between conflict resolution skills, relationship satisfaction, and the likelihood of divorce or separation (Epstein & Baucom, 1989; Gottman & Krakoff, 1989; Markman et al., 1988). Findings from the few studies to examine conflict resolution in lesbian and gay-male couples are mixed. For example, Kurdek (1991) found no differences in the problem-solving strategies used by lesbian and gay couples (Kurdek, 1991). However, in another study exploring conflict resolution patterns among gay, lesbian, and heterosexual couples, lesbians reported higher levels of satisfaction in their relationships and used more positive methods for resolving conflict than either gay male or heterosexual couples (Metz et al., 1995). Clearly, more research is needed to better understand conflict resolution strategies and relationship satisfaction among lesbian couples.

Consistent with previously reported studies (e.g., Bradford & Ryan, 1987; Hughes et al., 2000), lesbians in our sample were more likely than heterosexual women to have used mental health services. However, the proportion of lesbian and heterosexual respondents who sought mental health services in the previous five years to address relationship problems did not differ. Given the high rates of mental health use among lesbians in general, and the stressors faced by many lesbian couples, it is somewhat surprising that so few lesbians reported seeking therapy for relationship problems. Limited use of therapy for this purpose may reflect overall high levels of relationship satisfaction among lesbians studied. Alternatively, lesbians may be reluctant to report relationship problems because of low support and recognition given to lesbian relationships. Further, emotional problems, such as depression, may be a far stronger motivator for treatment than are relationship problems. It may also be the case that some lesbians do not disclose their same-sex relationships to health care providers–a factor that has important implications for quality of care.

CONCLUSIONS

These findings address several largely overlooked questions about lesbians' relationships and point to areas needing further investigation. For example, more information is needed about level of sexual activity among lesbians, the impact of discrepant sexual desire in lesbian couples, the types and effectiveness of conflict resolution strategies, and the factors contributing to lesbians' use of mental health services for relationship problems.

Although findings contribute to understanding about the similarities and differences between lesbians and heterosexual women in committed relationships, several limitations of the study must be noted. First, the sample was recruited using non-random, convenience methods. Women in this study were volunteer participants living in a large urban setting in the Midwest. Experiences of these women may differ substantially from those who live in rural areas, in areas that are more racial/ethnically homogeneous, or in areas where the larger population has less liberal attitudes toward gays and lesbians.

The sample size also limits generalizability of the findings and statistical power. Although the study sample was substantially more diverse than those included in most previous studies of lesbian health, the small sample size limited our ability to make comparisons based on race/ethnicity, socioeconomic status, or age, or to control for these variables in our analyses. Some differences between lesbians and heterosexual women would likely have been statistically significant had the sample been larger. Large-scale studies are needed to further examine the relationships reported here and to identify additional factors associated with healthy relationships among lesbians.

AUTHOR NOTE

This research was funded by the University of Illinois (UIC) Campus Research Board, the UIC College of Nursing Internal Research Support Program, and a developmental grant from the National Cancer Institute (awarded by the UIC Prevention Research Center). Development of this manuscript was supported by a research grant K01 AA00266 (Tonda L. Hughes, PI) from the National Institute on Alcohol Abuse and Alcoholism, National Institutes of Health. The instrument was developed for use in the National Study of Health and Life Experiences of Women, a national longitudinal study funded by the National Institute on Alcohol Abuse and Alcoholism, National Institutes of Health (R01 and R37 AA04610), Sharon C. Wilsnack, PI.

REFERENCES

Blumstein, P., & Schwartz, P. (1983). *American couples: Money, work and sex.* New York: Morrow.
Blumstein, P., & Schwartz, P. (1990). Intimate relationships and the creation of sexuality. In D.P. McWhirter, S.A. Sanders & J.M. Reinisch (Eds.), *Homosexuality/heterosexuality: Concepts of sexual orientation* (pp. 307-320). New York: Oxford University Press.

Bradford, J.B., & Ryan, C. (1987). *National lesbian health care survey: Mental health implications for lesbians* (Report No. PB88-201496/AS). Bethesda, MD: National Institute of Mental Health.

Caldwell, M.A., & Peplau, L.A. (1984). The balance of power in lesbian relationships. *Sex Roles, 10* (7/8), 587-599.

Chafetz, J.S. (1974). *Masculine/feminine or human: An overview of the sociology of sex roles.* Itasca, IL: Peacock.

Eldridge, N.S., & Gilbert, L.A. (1990). Correlates of relationship satisfaction in lesbian couples. *Psychology of Women Quarterly, 14*(1), 43-62.

Elliot, P. (1996). Shattering illusions: Same-sex domestic violence. In C.M. Renzetti, & C.H. Miley (Eds.), *Violence in gay and lesbian domestic partnerships* (pp. 1-8). Harrington Park Press.

Epstein, N., & Baucom, D.H. (1989). Cognitive-behavioral marital therapy. In A. Freeman, K.M. Simon, L.E. Beautle, & H. Arkowitz (Eds.), *Comprehensive handbook of cognitive therapy* (pp. 491-513). New York: Plenum.

Farley, N. (1996). A survey of factors contributing to gay and lesbian domestic violence. In C.M. Renzetti & C.H. Miley (Eds.), *Violence in gay and lesbian domestic partnerships* (pp. 35-42). Harrington Park Press.

Goglucci, N.M. (2000). Domestic violence in lesbian relationships. *Dissertation Abstracts International: Section B: The Sciences and Engineering, 60* (9-B), 4963.

Gottman, J.M., & Krakoff, L.J. (1989). Marital interaction and satisfaction: A longitudinal review. *Journal of Consulting and Clinical Psychology, 57*, 47-52.

Green, R.J., Bettinger, M., & Zacks, E. (1996). Are lesbian couples fused and gay male couples disengaged? Questioning gender straightjackets. In J. Laird & R.J. Green (Eds.), *Lesbians and gays in couples and families: A handbook for therapists.* (pp. 185-230). San Francisco, CA: Jossey-Bass Inc.

Greene, B., & Boyd-Franklin, N. (1996). African-American lesbians: Issues in couple's therapy. In J. Laird and R.J. Greene (Eds.), *Lesbians and gay men in couples and families: A handbook for therapists* (pp. 251-271). San Francisco: Jossey Bass.

Haas, S.M., & Stafford, L. (1998). An initial examination of maintenance behaviors in gay and lesbian relationships. *Journal of Social and Personal Relationships, 15* (6), 846-855.

Hughes, T.L., Haas, A.P., & Avery, L. (1997). Lesbians and mental health: Preliminary results from the Chicago women's health survey. *Journal of the Gay and Lesbian Medical Association, 1*, 133-144.

Hughes, T.L., Haas, A.P., Razzano, L., Cassidy, R., & Matthews, A. (2000). Comparing lesbians and heterosexual women's mental health: Results from a multi-site women's health survey. *Journal of Gay & Lesbian Social Services, 11*(1), 57-76.

Hughes, T.L., Johnson, T., & Wilsnack, S.C. (2001). Sexual assault and alcohol abuse: A comparison of lesbian and heterosexual women. *Journal of Substance Abuse.*

Kelly, J. (1972). Sister love: An exploration of the need for homosexual experience. *Family Coordinator, 21*(4), 473-475.

Klinkenberg, D., & Rose, S. (1994). Dating scripts of lesbians and gay men. *Journal of Homosexuality, 26*, 23-35.

Kotulski, D.S. (1996). *The expressions of love, sex, and intimacy in lesbian and heterosexual couples: A feminist inquiry. Dissertation Abstracts International: Section B: The Sciences and Engineering, 57* (6-B): 4090.

Kurdek, L.A., (1988). Relationship quality of gay and lesbian cohabitating couples. *Journal of Homosexuality, 15*, 93-118.

Kurdek, L.A. (1991). Correlates of relationship satisfaction in cohabitating gay and lesbian couples: Integration of contextual, investment, and problem-solving models. *Journal of Personality and Social Psychology, 56*, 910-922.

Kurdek, L.A., & Schmitt, J.P. (1986). Relationship quality of partners in heterosexual married, heterosexual cohabiting, and gay and lesbian relationships. *Journal of Personality and Social Psychology, 51*(4), 711-720.

Laumann, E.O., Gagnon, J.H., Michaels, R.T., & Michaels, S. (1994). *The social organization of sexuality: Sexual practices in the United States.* Chicago: University of Chicago Press.

Markman, H.J., Floyd, F.J., Stanley, S.M., & Storaasli, R.D. (1988). Prevention of marital distress: A longitudinal investigation. *Journal of Consulting and Clinical Psychology, 2*, 478-484.

Marrujo, B., & Kreger, M. (1996). Definition of roles in abusive lesbian relationships. In C.M. Renzetti & C.H. Miley (Eds.), *Violence in gay and lesbian domestic partnerships* (pp. 23-34). Harrington Park Press.

Metz, M.E., Rosser, Simon B.R., & Strapko, N. (1995). Differences in conflict-resolution styles among heterosexual, gay, and lesbian couples. *Journal of Sex Research, 31* (4), 293-308.

Morrow, S.K., & Hawxhurst, D.M. (1989). Lesbian partner abuse: Implications for therapists. *Journal of Counseling and Development, 68*, 31-35.

Nichols, M. (1988). Low sexual desire in lesbian couples. In S.R. Leiblum & R.C. Rosen (Eds.), *Sexual desire disorders* (pp. 387-412). New York, NY: Guilford Press.

Peplau, L.A., & Spalding, L.R. (2000). The close relationships of lesbians, gay men, and bisexuals. In C. Hendrick & S.S. Hendrick (Eds.), *Close relationships: A sourcebook* (pp. 111-124). Thousand Oaks, CA: Sage.

Renzetti, C. (1992). *Violent betrayal: Partner abuse in lesbian relationships.* Newbury Park, CA: Sage.

Schilit, R., Lie, G., & Montagne, M. (1991). Substance use as a correlate of violence in intimate lesbian relationships. *Journal of Homosexuality, 19* (3), 51-65.

Schreiner-Engel, P. (1986). *Clinical aspects of female sexuality.* Paper presented at the meeting of the International Academy of Sex Research, Amsterdam.

Seltzer, J.A., & Kalmuss, D. (1988). Socialization and stress explanations for spouse abuse. *Social Forces, 67*, 473-491.

Skrockie, F.E. (1996). *Use of focus groups to validate an existing instrument for use with lesbians.* Chicago: University of Illinois. Unpublished Master's Thesis.

Stark, E., & Flitcraft, A. (1988). Violence among intimates: An epidemiological review. In V.B. Van Hasselt, R.L. Morrison, A.S. Bellack, M. Hersen, & M. Hareway (Eds.), *Handbook of family violence* (pp. 293-318). New York: Plenum Press.

Waldner-Haugrud, L.K., Vaden Gratch, L., & Magruder, B. (1997). Victimization and perpetration rates of violence in gay and lesbian relationships: Gender issues explored. *Violence and Victims, 12*, 173-184.

Wilsnack, R.W., Wilsnack S.C., & Klassen A.D. (1984). Women's drinking and drinking problems: Patterns from a 1981 national survey. *American Journal of Public Health, 74*, 1231-1237.

Wilsnack, S.C., Klassen, A.D., Shur, B.E., & Wilsnack, R.W. (1991). Predicting onset and chronicity of women's problem drinking: A five-year longitudinal analysis. *American Journal of Public Health, 81*, 305-318.

Zacks, E., Green, R., & Morrow, J. (1988). Comparing lesbian and heterosexual couples on the circumplex model: An initial investigation. *Family Process, 27*, 471-484.

Internalized Homophobia in Lesbians

Dawn M. Szymanski

Y. Barry Chung

SUMMARY. In this article we discuss the importance of studying internalized homophobia and provide a rationale for studying internalized homophobia in lesbians apart from gay men. We review published scales used to assess internalized homophobia in lesbians and describe recent studies on the correlates of internalized homophobia in lesbians. We discuss concepts of internalized homophobia as minority stress and identify variables that have been theoretically linked to internalized homophobia in lesbians but have not been empirically examined. Implications for practice and research are also discussed. *[Article copies available for a fee from The Haworth Document Delivery Service: 1-800-HAWORTH. E-mail address: <getinfo@haworthpressinc.com> Website: <http://www.HaworthPress.com> © 2003 by The Haworth Press, Inc. All rights reserved.]*

KEYWORDS. Lesbians, internalized homophobia, mental health

Dawn M. Szymanski, PhD, is a post-doctoral Fellow at Georgia State University's counseling center and an adjunct professor at Argosy University/Atlanta (formerly Georgia School of Professional Psychology).

Y. Barry Chung, PhD, is Assistant Professor in the counseling psychology program at Georgia State University.

Address correspondence to: Dawn M. Szymanski, Counseling Center, Georgia State University, Atlanta, GA 30303-3083 (E-mail: dawnszymanski@msn.com).

[Haworth co-indexing entry note]: "Internalized Homophobia in Lesbians." Szymanski, Dawn M., and Y. Barry Chung. Co-published simultaneously in *Journal of Lesbian Studies* (Harrington Park Press, an imprint of The Haworth Press, Inc.) Vol. 7, No. 1, 2003, pp. 115-125; and: *Mental Health Issues for Sexual Minority Women: Redefining Women's Mental Health* (ed: Tonda L. Hughes, Carrol Smith, and Alice Dan) Harrington Park Press, an imprint of The Haworth Press, Inc., 2003, pp. 115-125. Single or multiple copies of this article are available for a fee from The Haworth Document Delivery Service [1-800-HAWORTH, 9:00 a.m. - 5:00 p.m. (EST). E-mail address: getinfo@haworthpressinc.com].

115

Weinberg (1972) coined the term homophobia to describe an irrational fear, intolerance, and hatred of homosexuality. Over the years, this definition has broadened to include the promotion and reinforcement of negative attitudes and images of lesbians and gay men in our culture, a belief system that justifies prejudice and discrimination based on sexual orientation, and the belief that heterosexuality is superior to homosexuality (Morin & Garfinkle, 1978; Pitman, 1999). "Internalized homophobia" represents lesbians' and gay men's inculcation of these negative attitudes and assumptions (Sophie, 1987), which often manifest themselves in subtle ways (Margolies, Becker, & Jackson-Brewer, 1987).

The terms homophobia and internalized homophobia have been criticized for being insufficient or inaccurate descriptors because of their narrow focus on the fear and avoidance of homosexuals, because they label the individual, not society, and because their connotation is pejorative (Herek, 1994, 2000). Several authors have proposed alternative terms such as "homonegativity" (Hudson & Ricketts, 1980), "homoprejudice" (Logan, 1996), and "sexual prejudice" (Herek, 2000). While there appears to be considerable merit in adopting a more accurate descriptor of internalized homophobia, this shift has not occurred in the majority of scholarly presentations and publications. In fact, all the empirical articles in this review used the term internalized homophobia rather than internalized homonegativity or some other term. Thus, we chose to use the term internalized homophobia and to give continued credit to the gay and lesbian pioneers who were instrumental in coining and promoting the construct it describes.

Shidlo (1994) listed four reasons why internalized homophobia is important: (1) it is suggested to be a developmental phenomenon that all lesbians and gay men experience to varying degrees as a result of living in a homophobic and heterosexist society; (2) it is associated with a variety of psychosocial problems, such as depression, low self-esteem, and difficulties developing and maintaining intimate relationships; (3) its examination and/or amelioration is often an important goal in therapy; and (4) it can serve a heuristic purpose, i.e., organizing factors unique to lesbians and gay men in the areas of psychosocial development, prevention of psychological distress, and counseling.

Although internalized homophobia appears to be equally important in the lives of both lesbians and gay men, internalized homophobia in lesbians should be examined separately for theoretical and practical reasons. De Monteflores and Schultz (1978) postulated that psychosocial differences between lesbians and gay men may have an impact on each group's identity formation. Unique factors affecting lesbian identity formation include effects of female gender-role socialization, repression of female sexual desire, experience of sexism in women's lives, and influences of the feminist movement (Faderman, 1984; McCarn & Fassinger, 1996; Roth, 1985; Vargo, 1987). Nungesser (1983) asserted that gender-role socialization contributes to differences in the rationalization for same-sex attraction and behavior between women and men. For example, a woman tends to avoid self-identification as a lesbian by emphasizing her feelings (e.g., "I really loved her"), while a man tends to cope by denying his feelings (e.g., "I was really drunk"). Men are socialized to be autonomous, differentiated, achievement oriented, competitive, and to make sexual conquests not necessarily associated with being in love (McClandish, 1982). In contrast, women are socialized to form relational identities and to interconnect autonomy and intimacy in their lives, which suggests that lesbians are more likely to "come out" in the context of a relationship rather than through acting on sexual desire alone. In addition, women are first taught to believe that sexual desire is improper, and then as lesbians that the objects of their desire are devalued and forbidden (McCarn & Fassinger, 1996). It is not possible to discuss the impact of internalized homophobia in lesbians without acknowledging the social, economic, political, and psychic costs of living in a woman-devaluing society (Greenfield, 1990). Thus, the negative effects of female socialization and internalized sexism are compounded in lesbians by internalized homophobia (Roth, 1985; Vargo, 1987).

The literature concerning internalized homophobia in lesbians focuses largely on the following topics: (1) instruments used in assessing internalized homophobia in lesbians, (2) correlates of internalized homophobia, (3) conceptualizations of internalized homophobia as minority stress, and (4) variables that have been theoretically linked to internalized homophobia in lesbians but have not been empirically examined.

ASSESSMENT OF INTERNALIZED HOMOPHOBIA IN LESBIANS

Scant empirical research exists on the assessment of internalized homophobia in lesbians. Only six published studies (Herek, Cogan, Gillis, & Glunt, 1997; Kahn, 1991; Lease, Cogdal, & Smith, 1995; McDermott, Tyndall, & Lichtenberg, 1989; McGregor et al., 2001; Radonsky & Borders, 1995) and a pilot study ($n = 17$; DiPlacido, 1998) were found that used more than one question in a survey to assess internalized homophobia. These studies are limited by their use of measures that focus on gay men, lack of theoretical support, lack of adequate reliability and/or validity, and/or focus on others' attitudes toward lesbians and gay men rather than on lesbians' and gay men's own feelings.

Recent advances in our knowledge of lesbian internalized homophobia have been made possible by the development of a new measure, the Lesbian Internalized Homophobia Scale (LIHS; Szymanski & Chung, 2001). Szymanski and Chung conceptualized lesbian internalized homophobia as consisting of five dimensions: (1) connection with the lesbian community (CLC), (2) public identification as a lesbian (PIL), (3) personal feelings about being a lesbian (PFL), (4) moral and religious attitudes toward lesbianism (MRATL), and (5) attitudes toward other lesbians (ATOL).

The CLC dimension refers to the extent to which a lesbian is connected to or separated from the larger lesbian community, and can range from isolation to social embeddedness. The PIL dimension refers to how a lesbian manages the disclosure of her identity, and can range from "passing" (i.e., looking like or talking as if one is heterosexual) and fear of discovery to identity disclosure. The PFL dimension refers to a lesbian's thoughts and reactions about being a lesbian, and can range from self-hatred to self-acceptance. The MRATL dimension refers to a lesbian's moral and religious beliefs, as they inform her attitudes about lesbianism and other lesbians, and can range from condemnation to tolerance and acceptance. The ATOL dimension refers to attitudes a lesbian holds about members of her own group, and can range from group deprecation to group appreciation.

The LIHS consists of 52 items assessing these five dimensions. Reliability and validity of scores on the scale have been supported in two studies of lesbians (Szymanski & Chung, 2001; Szymanski, Chung, & Balsam, 2001).

CORRELATES OF LESBIAN INTERNALIZED HOMOPHOBIA

Greater internalized homophobia has been found to be associated with traditional sex-role attitudes (i.e., beliefs about the appropriate roles of women in society) (Kahn, 1991); conflict concerning sexual orientation (Szymanski et al., 2001); lower levels of sexual orientation disclosure (Herek et al., 1997; McGregor et al., 2001; Radonsky & Borders, 1995; Szymanski et al., 2001); lack of connection to the lesbian/gay community and non-membership in a lesbian/gay/bisexual group (Herek et al., 1997; Szymanski et al., 2001); less overall social support, less gay social support, and less satisfaction with social support (McGregor et al., 2001; Szymanski et al., 2001); higher levels of demoralization (Herek et al., 1997); negative affect and greater alcohol consumption (DiPlacido, 1998); loneliness (Szymanski & Chung, 2001); and depression (Herek et al., 1997; Szymanski et al., 2001). In addition, DiPlacido (1998) found that sexual identity disclosure was associated with depression. Szymanski et al. (2001) found that a lack of connection with the lesbian community was associated with greater somatic complaints. Among lesbians treated for early stage breast cancer, internalized homophobia was associated with greater distress and less frequent Pap smears and gynecologic examinations (McGregor et al., 2001).

Mixed results have been found concerning the association between internalized homophobia and self-esteem. Szymanski and Chung (2001) found a positive relationship between the two variables (i.e., internalized homophobia was more pronounced in lesbians with low self-esteem), while Herek et al. (1997) and McGregor et al. (2001) found no significant relationship between internalized homophobia and self-esteem. Such inconsistent findings may be due to small sample sizes; the use of convenience samples that may not be representative of the lesbian population; skewed distributions and restricted range of scores on the internalized homophobia measures; uni-dimensional versus multi-dimensional conceptualization and assessment methods; and differences in the instruments used to assess internalized homophobia in lesbians.

Radonsky and Borders (1995) found no association between internalized homophobia and the people to whom a lesbian had disclosed her sexual orientation (i.e., other lesbians, gay men, non-gay men, non-gay women, and family members). Other research has found no association between internalized homophobia and stability of self-concept (Szymanski et al., 2001). Some research suggests that lesbians may have lower levels of internalized homophobia than gay men (Herek et al., 1997), and that attitudes toward *oneself* as a lesbian may be more closely related to psychosocial difficulties than are attitudes about *other* lesbians or lesbianism in general (Szymanski & Chung, 2001; Szymanski et al., 2001).

Two studies have examined the relationship between internalized homophobia and counseling expectancies and counselor preference among lesbians and gay men. McDermott et al. (1989) found that the degree of lesbians' and gay men's internalized homophobia was the best predictor of their overall comfort in discussing various concerns central to their sexual identity when they did not know their therapist's sexual orientation. Lease et al. (1995) found that lesbians and gay men with lower levels of internalized homophobia reported higher levels of personal commitment (openness, motivation, and responsibility) to the counseling process.

INTERNALIZED HOMOPHOBIA AS A COMPONENT OF MINORITY STRESS

Recently, internalized homophobia has been conceptualized as a component of minority stress. Building on the work of Brooks (1981), who described minority stress as psychological stress derived from minority status, Meyer (1995) conceptualized minority stressors as internalized homophobia, stigma, and experiences of anti-gay discrimination and violence. In a study of gay men, Meyer found support for hypotheses that these three stressors had independent negative associations with measures of psychological health. Similarly, DiPlacido (1998) conceptualized minority stressors as external stressors, such as daily hassles and negative events, and internal stressors as internalized homophobia, self-concealment, and emotional inhibition. She hypothesized that these minority stressors would be related to a variety of health behaviors and physical and psychological health outcomes in lesbians. Although findings from DiPlacido's pilot study appear promising, the results of her full study have not yet been published.

FEMINISM AND INTERNALIZED HOMOPHOBIA

The feminist movement advocates for the economic, social, legal, and political equality of women and men (Hirsch, Kett, & Trefil, 1993). It has facilitated the exploration of lesbianism through its philosophies and social analyses and through the development of resources, such as women's centers, feminist organizations, and feminist literature (Sophie, 1982). Additionally, feminist critiques of male domination and the institution of heterosexuality have legitimized lesbianism as a viable way of life for women (see, e.g., Rich, 1980). Graham, Rawlings, and Girten (1985; as cited in Kahn, 1991) postulated that a feminist ideology is one of the necessary pre-conditions for experiencing openness about one's lesbianism as psychologically healthy. A feminist ideology may supply some lesbians with pro-lesbian and pro-women attitudes that buffer or counteract experiences of internalized homophobia. Because feminism values woman-identified choices, women who self-identify as feminists may find it easier than non-feminists to develop a positive lesbian identity (Faderman, 1984; McCarn & Fassinger, 1996). Additionally, involvement in feminist activities may lessen a lesbian's internalized homophobia by providing her with opportunities to critically evaluate the institution of heterosexuality and societal norms, interact with self-affirming lesbians, and insulate her from societal homophobia (Faderman, 1984).

IMPLICATIONS FOR TREATMENT AND RESEARCH

As outlined in the literature review above, research findings suggest that internalized homophobia is associated with various psychosocial difficulties in lesbians. Research also suggests that the presence of social support, especially from other lesbians and gay men, may play an important role in combating internalized homophobia in lesbians (Szymanski et al., 2001). Additionally, theoretical links between internalized homophobia and feminism suggest that self-identification as a feminist, feminist attitudes, and involvement in feminist activities may also be important in mitigating lesbian internalized homophobia.

The findings discussed in this article highlight the importance of addressing internalized homophobia when working with lesbians in therapy. Mental health providers need to be able to determine the extent to which internalized homophobia influences the concerns that lesbians present with in therapy or counseling. Tools such as the LIHS can be used to encourage discussion of internalized homophobia.

When working on identity issues and internalized homophobia, therapists must help lesbian clients explore feelings free from evaluation or labeling, provide support and acceptance of same-sex feelings as well as worries and doubts about these feelings, and discourage the adoption of the label "lesbian" as long as that label has primarily negative meaning for the client (Sophie, 1982, 1987). Identifying and challenging negative stereotypes about lesbians can help lesbian clients achieve a positive identity (Gartrell, 1984; Padesky, 1988; Sophie, 1987). To facilitate clients' awareness and expression of these beliefs, therapists might say, "Most of us don't like to admit to having prejudices, but it is nearly impossible to grow up in this society without being taught negative things about lesbians and other minority groups. What are some of the things you've been taught about lesbians?" (Padesky, 1988, p. 148). Once negative beliefs and stereotypes about lesbians have been identified, cognitive methods can be used to help clients test these beliefs and evaluate their validity. Providing factual information about lesbianism can be beneficial (Gartrell, 1984). Additionally, contact with other lesbians and gay men can facilitate positive beliefs about homosexuality and about lesbians and provide important social support (Gartrell, 1984; Sophie, 1982, 1987; Szymanski et al., 2001).

When assessing environmental effects and internalized beliefs, a feminist perspective can be especially useful (Falco, 1991). Suggested strategies include providing a feminist analysis of sexuality, heterosexual privilege, homophobia, sexism, and gender roles; facilitating an awareness of how social class, race, ethnicity, age, and other demographic factors interact to influence homophobia; facilitating an examination of the impact of cultural oppression on psychological functioning; and discussing the possibility of involvement in social change efforts aimed at eliminating prejudice, bias, and discrimination based on sexual orientation (Brown, 1988; Neisen, 1993; Sophie, 1982).

SUGGESTIONS FOR FUTURE RESEARCH

A number of variables have been theoretically linked to internalized homophobia in lesbians (e.g., internalized misogyny, alcohol and other drug abuse, problems with intimacy), but have not been adequately studied (Brown, 1986; Brown, 1987; DiPlacido, 1998; Faderman, 1984; Falco, 1991; Glaus, 1988; Margolies, Becker, & Jackson-Brewer, 1987; McCarn & Fassinger, 1996; Nichols, 1983; Pharr, 1988; Pitman, 1999; Roth, 1985; Sophie, 1982; Vargo, 1987; Zevy & Cavallaro, 1987). Research is also needed to examine variables that have been correlated with internalized homophobia in gay men, such as distrust, relationship satisfaction, fear of intimacy, gender roles, psychological distress, and coping style (Frederick, 1995; Nicholson & Long, 1990; Ross & Rosser, 1996; Shidlo, 1994), to determine if similar relationships exist among lesbians. Studies are especially needed to better understand internalized homophobia across different groups of sexual minority women. For example, how does the perception of stigma and sexual identity disclosure differ in lesbians and bisexual women and do the relationships between these variables and internalized homophobia differ for lesbians and bisexual women? How does internalized homophobia differ among women with multiple marginalized statuses such as racial/ethnic minorities and women with disabilities? Cross-cultural studies would be helpful for understanding the interrelationships between stigma, cultural mores, and internalized homophobia. Finally, research is needed to identify coping strategies and resources that may mitigate internalized homophobia and related psychosocial difficulties in lesbians as well as on the effectiveness of counseling interventions aimed at reducing internalized homophobia in lesbians.

In conclusion, research findings suggest that lesbian internalized homophobia is related to a variety of psychosocial difficulties and may impede the counseling process. Mental health providers can play an important role in helping lesbian clients recognize and deal with internalized homophobia and develop a positive lesbian identity. Future research exploring variables that have been theoretically linked to internalized homophobia in lesbians but have not yet been empirically tested is encouraged.

REFERENCES

Brooks, V.R. (1981). *Minority stress and lesbian women.* Lexington, MA: D. C. Heath.
Brown, L.S. (1986). Confronting internalized oppression in sex therapy with lesbians. *Journal of Homosexuality, 12,* 99-107.

Brown, L.S. (1987). Lesbians, weight, and eating: New analyses and perspectives. In Boston Lesbian Psychologies Collective (Ed.), *Lesbian psychologies: Explorations and challenges* (pp. 294-309). Chicago, IL: University of Illinois Press.

Brown, L.S. (1988). Feminist therapy with lesbians and gay men. In M.A. Dutton-Douglas & L.E.A. Walker (Eds.), *Feminist psychotherapies: Integration of therapeutic and feminist systems* (pp. 206-227). Norwood, NJ: Ablex Publishing.

de Monteflores, C., & Schultz, S.J. (1978). Coming out: Similarities and differences for lesbians and gay men. *Journal of Social Issues, 34*(3), 59-72.

DiPlacido, J. (1998). Minority stress among lesbians, gay men, and bisexuals: A consequence of heterosexism, homophobia, and stigmatization. In G.M. Herek (Ed.), *Stigma and sexual orientation: Understanding prejudice against lesbians, gay men, and bisexuals* (pp. 138-159). Thousand Oaks, CA: Sage Publications.

Faderman, L. (1984). The "new gay" lesbians. *Journal of Homosexuality, 10*(3/4), 85-97.

Falco, K.L. (1991). *Psychotherapy with lesbian clients: Theory into practice.* New York: Brunner/Mazel.

Frederick, R.J. (1995). *Internalized homophobia, gender roles, self-esteem and fear of intimacy in gay men.* Unpublished doctoral dissertation, Fairleigh Dickinson University.

Gartrell, N. (1984). Combating homophobia in the psychotherapy of lesbians. *Women & Therapy, 3*, 13-29.

Glaus, O.K. (1988). Alcoholism, chemical dependency, and the lesbian client. *Women & Therapy, 8*, 131-144.

Greenfield, F.M. (1990). *Internalized homophobia in lesbians: A preliminary investigation of construct validity.* Unpublished master's thesis, Georgia State University, Atlanta, GA.

Herek, G.M. (1994). Assessing heterosexuals' attitudes toward lesbians and gay men: A review of empirical research with the ATLG scale. In B. Greene & G.M. Herek (Eds.), *Lesbian and gay psychology: Theory, research and clinical applications* (pp. 206-228). Thousand Oaks, CA: Sage Publications.

Herek, G.M. (2000). The psychology of sexual prejudice. *Current Directions in Psychological Science, 9*(1), 19-22.

Herek, G.M., Cogan, J.C., Gillis, J.R., & Glunt, E.K. (1997). Correlates of internalized homophobia in a community sample of lesbians and gay men. *Journal of the Gay and Lesbian Medical Association, 2*, 17-25.

Hirsh, E.D., Kett, J.F., & Trefil, J. (1993). *The dictionary of cultural literacy.* Boston, MA: Houghton Mifflin Company.

Hudson, W., & Ricketts, W.A. (1980). A strategy for measurement of homophobia. *Journal of Homosexuality, 5*, 357-371.

Kahn, M.J. (1991). Factors affecting the coming out process for lesbians. *Journal of Homosexuality, 21*(3), 47-70.

Lease, S.H., Cogdal, P.A., & Smith, D. (1995). Counseling expectancies related to counselor's sexual orientation and clients' internalized homophobia. *Journal of Gay & Lesbian Psychotherapy, 2*(3), 51-65.

Logan, C. (1996). Homophobia? No, homoprejudice. *Journal of Homosexuality, 31*, 31-53.

Margolies, L., Becker, M., & Jackson-Brewer, K. (1987). Internalized homophobia: Identifying and treating the oppressor within. In Boston Lesbian Psychologies Collective (Ed.), *Lesbian psychologies: Explorations and challenges* (pp. 229-241). Urbana, IL: University of Illinois Press.

McCarn, S.R., & Fassinger, R.E. (1996). Revisioning sexual minority identity formation: A new model of lesbian identity and its implications for counseling and research. *The Counseling Psychologist, 24*, 508-534.

McClandish, B. (1982). Therapeutic issues with lesbian couples. In J. Gonsiorek (Ed.), *Homosexuality and psychotherapy: A practitioner's handbook of affirmative models* (pp. 71-78). New York: The Haworth Press, Inc.

McDermott, D., Tyndall, L., & Lichtenberg, J.W. (1989). Factors related to counselor preference among gays and lesbians. *Journal of Counseling and Development, 68,* 31-35.

McGregor, B.A., Carver, C.S., Antoni, M.H., Weiss, S., Yount, S.E., & Ironson, G. (2001). Distress and internalized homophobia among lesbian women treated for early stage breast cancer. *Psychology of Women Quarterly, 25*, 1-9.

Meyer, I.H. (1995). Minority stress and mental health in gay men. *Journal of Health and Social Behavior, 36*, 38-56.

Morin, S.F., & Garfinkle, E.M. (1978). Male homophobia. *Journal of Social Issues, 34,* 29-47.

Neisen, J.H. (1993). Healing from cultural victimization: Recovery from shame due to heterosexism. *Journal of Gay & Lesbian Psychotherapy, 2*(1), 49-63.

Nichols, M. (1983). The treatment of inhibited sexual desire (ISD) in lesbian couples. *Women & Therapy, 1*(4), 49-66.

Nicholson, W.D., & Long, B.C. (1990). Self-esteem, social support, internalized homophobia, and coping strategies of HIV+ gay men. *Journal of Consulting and Clinical Psychology, 58*, 873-876.

Nungesser, L.G. (1983). *Homosexual acts, actors, and identities.* New York: Praeger.

Padesky, C.A. (1988). Attaining and maintaining positive lesbian self-identity: A cognitive therapy approach. *Women & Therapy, 8*(1/2), 145-156.

Pharr, S. (1988). *Homophobia: A weapon of sexism.* Little Rock, AR: Chardon Press.

Pitman, G.E. (1999). Body image, compulsory heterosexuality, and internalized homophobia. *Journal of Lesbian Issues, 3*(4), 129-139.

Radonsky, V.E., & Borders, L.D. (1995). Factors influencing lesbians' direct disclosure of their sexual orientation. *Journal of Gay & Lesbian Psychotherapy, 2*(3), 17-37.

Rich, A. (1980). Compulsory heterosexuality and lesbian existence. *Signs: Journal of Women in Culture and Society, 5*, 631-660.

Ross, M.W., & Rosser, B.R. (1996). Measurement and correlates of internalized homophobia: A factor analytic study. *Journal of Clinical Psychology, 52*(1), 15-21.

Roth, S. (1985). Psychotherapy with lesbian couples: Individual issues, female socialization, and the social context. *Journal of Marital and Family Therapy, 11*, 273-286.

Shidlo, A. (1994). Internalized homophobia: Conceptual and empirical issues in measurement. In B. Greene & G.M. Herek (Eds.), *Lesbian and gay psychology: Theory, research and clinical applications* (pp. 176-205). Thousand Oaks, CA: Sage Publications.

Sophie, J. (1982). Counseling lesbians. *Personnel and Guidance Journal, 60,* 341-345.

Sophie, J. (1987). Internalized homophobia and lesbian identity. *Journal of Homosexuality, 14,* 53-65.

Szymanski, D.M., & Chung, Y.B. (2001). The Lesbian Internalized Homophobia Scale: A rational/theoretical approach. *Journal of Homosexuality, 41*(2), 37-52.

Szymanski, D.M., Chung, Y.B., & Balsam, K. (2001). Psychosocial correlates of internalized homophobia in lesbians. *Measurement and Evaluation in Counseling and Development, 34,* 27-38.

Vargo, S. (1987). The effects of women's socialization on lesbian couples. In Boston Lesbian Psychologies Collective (Ed.), *Lesbian psychologies: Explorations and challenges* (pp. 161-174). Boston, MA: University of Chicago Press.

Weinberg, G. (1972). *Society and the healthy homosexual.* Boston, MA: Alyson.

Zevy, L., & Cavallaro, S.A. (1978). Invisibility, fantasy, and intimacy: Princess charming is not prince. In Boston Lesbian Psychologies Collective (Ed.), *Lesbian psychologies: Explorations and challenges* (pp. 83-94). Urbana, IL: University of Illinois Press.

Sexual Minorities Seeking Services: A Retrospective Study of the Mental Health Concerns of Lesbian and Bisexual Women

Tracey L. Rogers
Kristen Emanuel
Judith Bradford

SUMMARY. Understanding the mental health needs of lesbian and bisexual (sexual minority) women is an integral part of designing and providing appropriate mental health services and treatment for them. In an effort to understand the mental health needs of sexual minority women who seek community treatment, a chart review was conducted of the 223 lesbian and bisexual women who presented for services between July 1, 1997 and December 31, 2000 at Fenway Community Health in Boston, MA. Data are based on clients' self-reports and clinician assessments of clients' presenting problem, relevant developmental history, prior men-

Tracey L. Rogers, PhD, is Manager of Behavioral Research, Department of Research and Evaluation, Fenway Community Health, Boston, MA.

Kristen Emanuel, MTS, is affiliated with Fenway Community Health, Boston, MA.

Judith Bradford, PhD, is affiliated with the Survey and Evaluation Research Laboratory, Richmond, VA, and with Fenway Community Health.

Address correspondence to: Tracey Rogers, PhD, Fenway Community Health, 7 Haviland Street, Boston, MA 02215 (E-mail: Trogers@fenwayhealth.org).

[Haworth co-indexing entry note]: "Sexual Minorities Seeking Services: A Retrospective Study of the Mental Health Concerns of Lesbian and Bisexual Women." Rogers, Tracey L., Kristen Emanuel, and Judith Bradford. Co-published simultaneously in *Journal of Lesbian Studies* (Harrington Park Press, an imprint of The Haworth Press, Inc.) Vol. 7, No. 1, 2003, pp. 127-146; and: *Mental Health Issues for Sexual Minority Women: Redefining Women's Mental Health* (ed: Tonda L. Hughes, Carrol Smith, and Alice Dan) Harrington Park Press, an imprint of The Haworth Press, Inc., 2003, pp. 127-146. Single or multiple copies of this article are available for a fee from The Haworth Document Delivery Service [1-800-HAWORTH, 9:00 a.m. - 5:00 p.m. (EST). E-mail address: getinfo@haworthpressinc.com].

tal health and substance abuse treatment, current reports of emotional/ psychological symptoms, and areas of impaired functioning. Although substance abuse and suicidal ideation were commonly reported problems, other concerns were more frequently reported. High percentages of lesbians and bisexual women reported relationship concerns and lack of adequate social networks; rates of depression and anxiety based on clinicians' assessments were also high. Overall, lesbians and bisexual women did not differ in the issues they brought to treatment or level or types of impairment. Compared with previous community survey samples, however, study participants appeared to be healthier than general, non-clinical samples of self-identified lesbians, possibly reflecting the special characteristics of sexual minority women who seek treatment in specialized community sites such as the Fenway. Although patients who come to these sites may not represent the more general population of sexual minority women, community health centers known to serve lesbian, gay, bisexual and transgender (LGBT) individuals may be fruitful access points for studying the mental health status and treatment needs of sexual minority women. *[Article copies available for a fee from The Haworth Document Delivery Service: 1-800-HAWORTH. E-mail address: <getinfo@haworthpressinc.com> Website: <http://www.HaworthPress. com> © 2003 by The Haworth Press, Inc. All rights reserved.]*

KEYWORDS. Mental health services, lesbians, bisexual women, depression, anxiety

Lesbian and bisexual women, by virtue of being sexual minorities in our society, face unique stressors that include prejudice, stigmatization, antigay violence and internalization of negative social attitudes (Herek, Gillis & Cogen, 1999). Although research on lesbian and bisexual women's mental health is growing and its importance is increasingly recognized, it is as yet unclear how these stressors impact the mental health and needs of this population of women. A 1999 report on lesbian health from the Institute of Medicine (IOM) noted as its first priority the need for research to better understand the mental and physical health status of lesbians and to identify risk and protective factors affecting lesbians' mental health (Solarz, 1999). Additional research is also essential to the development of effective mental health treatment, prevention programs, and public health policies to meet the needs of this population.

Sexual minority women often face significant barriers in obtaining access to quality health care (Bradford & White, 2000). An earlier IOM report presented a conceptual framework for understanding the challenges of providing care to underserved populations, categorizing barriers as structural, financial, and personal/cultural (Millman, 1993). Sexual minority women, especially those who have low incomes, live in rural areas, and/or have limited facility with English, may face structural or financial barriers similar to members of any underserved population (U.S. Department of Health and Human Services, 2000). Simply by virtue of being lesbian or bisexual, these women face additional barriers related to their own personal and cultural characteristics, as well as characteristics of their providers (Scout et al., 2001). In previous research, lesbians have been shown to seek care less often than recommended and to be inadequately informed about their health care needs (Bradford & White, 2000). Medical and mental health providers report negative attitudes toward sexual minority women, as well as a lack of knowledge about lesbianism and the specific, unique needs of lesbian and bisexual women, which too often translates into inadequate care (Bradford, Ryan, Honnold & Rothblum, 2001; Ryan et al., 1999). For sexual minority women, the results can be devastating, even life-threatening.

Models of optimal care for sexual minority women are currently unavailable, although a preliminary set of "best practices" can be developed from recommendations in published literature and research reports. Core concepts for culturally sensitive health care practices were included in the IOM report on lesbian health (Solarz, 1999) and have been reported at conferences and in monographs. Standards of practice have been developed in at least two states for health care to lesbian, gay, bisexual, and transgender (LGBT) persons, further expanding the thinking in this direction (Clark, Landers, Linde & Sperber, 2001). Emerging best practices center upon the need to increase health literacy among LGBT individuals and their providers and to identify and reduce the LGBT-negative, often homophobic environments that exist within many health care organizations.

A national network of community health centers serving the LGBT community has increased its collaborative efforts to develop optimal health care to sexual-minority lesbians and, in conjunction with academic and community researchers, has begun to organize consortia and multi-site studies (Bradford, Rogers, Rice & Roberts, 2001). Several of these centers are working intentionally with each other and collaborating researchers to articulate best practices for research and care to lesbian and bisexual women and to improve access to more culturally sensitive systems of care. Fenway Community Health (FCH or "the Fenway") in Boston, MA, the site at which data reported in this paper were collected, is one of 10 LGBT health centers making up a special group of community access points that can increase access to quality health care for many lesbians and bisexual women.

A necessary part of developing best practices is obtaining a better understanding of the needs of those who come to LGBT centers. FCH was considered uniquely situated to begin this exploration because it has provided medical and mental health care to the LGBT community for 30 years and initiated a health care and research program for lesbian and bisexual women in 1989 (Carroll, Linde, Mayer, Lara & Bradford, 1999; Mayer et al., 2001). In this paper, we present results of a mental health chart review conducted in 2001 at the Fenway to explore the mental health status and treatment needs of 223 lesbian and bisexual minority women who sought care between July 1, 1997 and December 31, 2000. The chart review reported here is a component of FCH's efforts to translate research findings into practice models. It was anticipated that results would assist FCH providers to review, and if needed, modify the care offered to sexual minority women.

PREVIOUS RESEARCH

Most previous research efforts to clarify the service needs of sexual minority women have relied upon non-probability samples to assess the mental health needs of the lesbian/bisexual community at large and/or to compare the proportion of lesbians and bisexual women who self-report mental health concerns with prevalence rates for women in the adult general population. Bradford, Ryan and Rothblum (1994), Trippet (1994), and Gambrill, Stein and Brown (1984) all included questions about mental health concerns and service needs on general health surveys of lesbians and bisexual women, and reported that among the most common mental health concerns of their study participants were relationship issues, issues related to disclosure of sexual orientation, and self-reported depression. Findings from these studies also highlight the role that social stigma plays in the mental health concerns of lesbians (GLMA, 2000). In a more recent study, Morris, Waldo and Rothblum (2001) found that 41% of their national sample reported thoughts of suicide, and 21.5% had attempted suicide at least once in their lifetime.

Other studies have used community sample surveys to compare the self-reported mental health concerns of lesbians or bisexual women with prevalence rates reported for women in the general population. Although direct comparisons can be problematic, self-reported concerns consistently suggest that the psychological adjustment of non-clinical samples of lesbians does not differ from that of heterosexual women as measured by population-based studies (McKirnan & Peterson, 1989; Rothblum & Factor, 2001). Self-reported depression was the most common mental health issue for the National Lesbian Health Care Study (NLHCS) participants—a finding suggested by the study's researchers to be comparable to prevalence data on adult women in the general U.S. population, gathered at the same time period through the National Health

Interview Survey (NHIS). In contrast, Cochran and Mays' (1994) survey of homosexually active African American men and women found levels of depression to be higher than would be expected on the basis of race, gender or sexual orientation alone.

Community survey findings are also inconsistent with prevalence data regarding substance abuse and suicide among sexual minority women. Summarizing data from a wide range of non-probability sample studies from the 1970s and 1980s, authors of the 1999 IOM report found that as many as 30% of lesbians were heavy drinkers or had alcohol-related problems. These results suggested that alcohol abuse is a problem for which lesbians appear to be at greater risk than heterosexual women (Solarz, 1999). In more recent studies, however, lesbians have self-reported rates of heavy drinking comparable to those of heterosexual women, yet tend to report more alcohol-related problems (Bloomfield, 1993; Hughes, Haas, Razzano, Cassidy & Matthews, 2000; Hughes, Johnson & Wilsnack, 2001; McKirnan & Peterson, 1989).

Self-reported frequency of attempted suicide among lesbians has also varied from one study to another, further illustrating the inherent limitations of non-probability studies for understanding the range and seriousness of these events. More than one-half the NLHCS sample reported thoughts of suicide and 18% had attempted suicide at some time in their lives, compared to rates of 33% and 4% respectively for adult general population women in the Epidemiology Catchment Area (ECA) studies (as cited in GLMA, 2000). However, a review of suicide research in the recent Healthy People 2010 Companion Document for LGBT Health (GLMA, 2000) suggests that although lesbians, like gay men, appear to be at greater risk for lifetime prevalence of suicidal ideation and suicide attempts, insufficient evidence exists to document heightened risk for completed suicide.

Recent studies of lesbians' mental health that have employed more sophisticated methodologies provide important data about the prevalence of mental health disorders. Results from more rigorous studies provide sounder comparisons with rates among other groups such as women and men in the general population, gay men, and the heterosexual sisters of lesbians. The Netherlands Mental Health Survey and Incidence Study (NEMESIS) used data from a multistage, stratified, random sample of households in The Netherlands to compare homosexually active women and men with heterosexually active women and men (Sandfort, deGraaf, Bijl & Schnabel, 2001) and found that homosexually active women and men were more likely to have mood and anxiety disorders than were their heterosexually active counterparts. The authors also found that homosexually active women were more likely than heterosexually active women to have a lifetime prevalence of more than one psychiatric disorder. On the other hand, in a study of sexual minority women from the 1996 National

Household Survey of Drug Abuse, Cochran and Mays (2000) found that although women who reported same gender partners in the previous year were more likely than other women to evidence drug or alcohol dependency, they were no more likely to meet criteria for other psychiatric disorders such as major depression, generalized anxiety, agoraphobia and panic. Similarly, a study comparing 184 pairs of lesbians and their heterosexual sisters found no significant differences between the two groups on measures assessing the prevalence and severity of mental disorders (Rothblum & Factor, 2001).

Despite the substantial increase in the number of studies addressing the mental health of sexual minorities in the past five years, there continues to be a need for empirical data on lesbians' mental health. Population-level information is particularly helpful in determining whether certain disorders occur more or less frequently among sexual minorities than among heterosexuals, but more research is needed to better understand the mental health needs of sexual minority women who actually seek treatment. The present study was undertaken to describe the treatment needs of sexual minority women who presented for treatment at Fenway Community Health (FCH), a specialized community-based health organization devoted to the treatment of sexual minorities. Understanding this population's mental health needs is a necessary first step in determining whether services offered are those most needed by clients served by the Center.

METHODS

Clinical Setting and Sample

Fenway Community Health is the largest lesbian/gay/bisexual/transgender health center in New England, unique in its delivery of comprehensive LGBT health services and its development of model programs for the community. In addition to the medical and mental health services that have been offered since its founding in 1971, FCH services address broader community concerns, including substance use, parenting issues, domestic and homophobic violence, and other specialized needs of lesbians, bisexuals and transgendered individuals. An acupuncture detoxification program has been in operation at FCH since 1989.

FCH has provided health services to lesbians since its inception in 1971. In 1980, mental health and addiction services for lesbians were initiated, including individual and couples' psychotherapy and support groups. Family and parenting services were first offered in 1983, allowing FCH to offer home- and office-based inseminations. The establishment of the Women's Health Task Force in the late 1980s gave impetus and direction to the expansion of services for women, helping launch and support special events and health promotion/education programs that helped attract lesbian clients. Although other social service agencies and treatment programs in the Boston area welcome and serve sexual minority women, no other agency's mission or programs are designed explicitly to serve this population.

Data for this study were gathered from all women who presented for mental health services at FCH between July 1997 and December 2000. A total of 322 women were seen in Fenway's mental health department during the 42-month study period, of whom 91 (28%) self-identified as heterosexual, 191 (59%) as lesbian, and 32 (10%) as bisexual.

DATA COLLECTION AND ANALYSIS

To conduct the study, we created an individualized record for each patient, linking electronic medical record data with chart review information. Mental health intakes at FCH consist of one- to three-hour clinical interviews conducted by psychologists and social workers. All clients who present for mental health services have an intake interview, and all treatment recommendations and assignments are based on this interview. The clinicians obtain a complete history of clients' presenting problems; relevant developmental history; prior medical, mental health and substance abuse treatment; sexual behavior; current symptoms; and areas of impaired functioning. Intake data are based on multiple sources of information. Some domains, such as symptoms and functioning, are self-report, whereas others, such as diagnoses and assessment of substance abuse, rely on clinician judgment. Clinicians then enter all information obtained at intake into Logician, the computerized medical record system used for all medical and mental health services at FCH. Logician contains the templates for each department's standard intake and visit forms and intakes are not considered complete until all sections of the form are completed. Clinical supervisors are required to review and make a determination about the completeness of all intakes.

Two researchers extracted information from records using a chart review questionnaire developed specifically for this study. This questionnaire focused on specific domains and provided a standardized way of collecting data from the charts regarding age, race/ethnicity, sexual orientation, age of awareness of lesbian or bisexual orientation, employment status, zip code, and insurance status. Information was also obtained on the following clinical dimensions: presenting problem, history of substance abuse, familial history of substance abuse, history of physical, sexual or emotional abuse, assessments of impaired functioning and current symptomatology, and previous mental health and substance abuse treatment. Finally, the review noted clients' diagnoses based on the American Psychiatric Association's Diagnostic and Statistical Manual of Mental Disorders (DSM-IV, APA, 1994). At intake clinicians ask about many sensitive issues (e.g., physical and/or sexual trauma, drug and alcohol use) that clients may not disclose during an initial contact. Because the data reflect only information gathered at intake, it may therefore underestimate the prevalence of some mental health concerns.

Care was taken to maintain confidentiality of patient records. All forms and study-related materials were numerically coded and secured in locked file cabinets and access to these file cabinets was limited to research personnel conducting the study. Institutional Review Board (IRB) approval was sought and obtained for this review of records. All information from the chart review tool was entered into Microsoft Access. Statistical analyses were performed using SPSS. This paper reports data describing the presenting mental health concerns of sexual minority women. While results of chi-square analyses comparing the lesbians and bisexual women are reported, these results need to be interpreted with caution given the large difference in the size of the two groups (191 lesbians, 32 bisexual women).

Study data have several unusual strengths. Clinicians at FCH are sensitive to the importance of sexual orientation and are trained to routinely inquire about this aspect of clients' lives, unlike most clinical settings where staff may not even ask about sexual orientation. With clinicians having "opened the door," clients often feel more comfortable discussing the impact of sexual orientation on their lives. Unlike most studies that report data collected only from lesbians, we also report findings from bisexual women and compare data from lesbians and bisexual women to explore similarities or differences in treatment and prevention needs. Because a computerized record system consisting of numerous measures and clinical information has been in place at FCH since July 1997, available information from mental health intakes represents an unusually rich source of data.

Measures

Counseling and Therapy History. As part of the intake interview, clinicians gather information about previous treatment including medical treatment as well as mental health and substance abuse treatment. Data for this variable were coded "yes" or "no" indicating whether the client had ever received treatment for a mental health or for a substance abuse-related problem.

Symptoms and Functioning. The FCH intake form contains two clinician-administered inventories: (1) a checklist of 22 symptoms (e.g., anxiety, hopelessness, decreased energy) that the client is *currently* experiencing, and (2) a list of 13 areas of functioning (e.g., marriage and family relationships, ability to concentrate). The symptom checklist, developed by clinicians experienced in the assessment of mental disorders, includes symptoms from each of the major DSM IV (APA, 1994) categories of mental disorders. The functioning checklist samples domains of life in which impairment is most commonly associated with mental disorder. Neither the symptom nor functioning checklists are standardized measures.

Suicidal Ideation. At intake, all clients are asked if they currently have thoughts of suicide, if they have a plan to commit suicide, and if so, whether they have the means to carry out the plan. Clients are also asked about past (lifetime) suicidal thoughts or attempts. Suicidal ideation is coded as being present if a client reports suicidal thoughts or a plan to commit suicide.

Substance Abuse. Clinicians gather a thorough substance use history, including past and current substance use, the impact of use on functioning, and substance abuse treatment. Although an inventory of current and lifetime use of substances is obtained, assessments of substance *abuse* are made by clinicians based on DSM-IV criteria for substance abuse, using clients' self-report of problems and/or indications of impaired functioning related to substance use.

Psychiatric Diagnoses. After completing the intake interview clinicians are expected to integrate the information they have received and make a diagnosis, based on criteria from the Diagnostic and Statistical Manual of Mental Disorders–IV (DSM-IV; APA, 1994). The DSM-IV multiaxial system assesses medical conditions, psychosocial and environmental problems, level of functioning, and mental disorders. The diagnoses we report were made based on clinical judgment using the criteria outlined for each disorder. We report Axis I and IV disorders. Axis I is used to report clinical disorders or conditions that are the focus of clinical attention (e.g., major depression or generalized anxiety disorder). As such, Axis I provides the best description of a client's current state and reason for seeking treatment. Axis IV is used to report psychosocial and environmental problems that may affect diagnosis, treatment, and prognosis. This Axis is important for identifying problems that shape the context in which a person's difficulties have developed (e.g., death of a parent or recent surgery). Although Axis II, which is used to report on personality disorders or maladaptive personality features, represents an important clinical dimension, these diagnoses are best made after repeated contact with a client. Thus, we focus on the Axis I and IV because they best describe the reasons clients present for treatment.

RESULTS

Description of the Sample

Table 1 summarizes the demographic characteristics of our sample. A total of 322 individual women patients were seen during the study period, of whom

TABLE 1. Sample Demographics

	Sexual Minorities n = 223	
	N	%
Sexual Orientation:		
Lesbian	191	86%
Heterosexual		
Bisexual	32	14%
Transgender		
Other		
Race/Ethnicity:		
Caucasian	185	83%
African American	21	9.4%
Hispanic	9	4.0%
Asian/Pacific Islander/Native	5	2.2%
Unknown	3	1.4%
Age:		
Under 20	2	.1%
20-29 years old	57	25.5%
30-39 years old	91	40.8%
40-49 years old	51	22.8%
50 or over	22	9.8%
Employment:		
Full-Time	138	61.8%
Student	34	15.3%
Unemployed	24	10.7%
Disabled	11	4.9%
Part-Time	7	3.2%
Other	9	4.1%
Age of GLBT Awareness: **		
< 12 years old/always	27	12.1%
12-18 years old	31	13.9%
19-29 years old	48	21.5%
30 years or older	17	7.6%

**Data on this variable was only available on 45% of the sample due to clinician variation in collecting this information. Percentages are based on the 123 women for whom this information was available.

223 (70%) self-identified as lesbian or bisexual. Most of the sexual minority women (86%, n = 191) self-identified as lesbian, and 14% (n = 32) self-identified as bisexual. A large majority (83%) were Caucasian; 9% were African American, 4% Hispanic, and the remainder were Asian/Pacific Islander, Native American, multiracial, or of some other race/ethnicity. Patients in the study population were most likely to be between 30-39 years of age (40%).

Two-thirds (66%) were not in a committed relationship with a woman or man; 14% had children.

Lesbians and bisexual patients differed from heterosexual women patients in age and employment status. Heterosexual women are excluded from analyses because the two groups differed significantly on two key demographic variables. Heterosexual women were younger than sexual minority women, ($\chi^2(6) = 24.966$, p = .000) and less likely to be employed ($\chi^2 (2) = 24.293$, p = .000). These figures reflect the fact that one of the populations served by the health center are the college students at schools in the Fenway neighborhood. Because of the impact of these characteristics on patterns of health status and access to health care, no further comparisons were made with heterosexual women. Instead, this paper focuses on the mental health status and treatment needs of sexual minority women only, comparing lesbians to bisexual women when data make this feasible. Lesbian and bisexual women differed on several key demographic variables. Bisexual women were more likely than lesbians to be Caucasian ($\chi^2 (1) = 5.336$, p = .025), and were younger ($\chi^2 (6) = 21.326$, p = .002). Bisexual women were also more likely than lesbians to be employed ($\chi^2 (2) = 7.398$, p = .025).

Counseling and Therapy History. An overwhelming majority of both lesbian and bisexual women reported prior use of mental health services; most reported outpatient treatment for a mental health concern (83% of lesbians and 81% of bisexual women). Fewer lesbians (18%) and bisexual women (13%) reported inpatient treatment for a mental health problem. Similarly, relatively few lesbians (13%) or bisexual women (9%) reported having received treatment for substance abuse.

Symptoms and Functioning. Tables 2 and 3 summarize data concerning symptoms and functioning reported by lesbians and bisexual women in the sample. Depression (87%) and anxiety (81%) were the most commonly reported symptoms. More than 40% reported decreased energy, grief and irritability. In terms of functioning, the area where problems were most commonly reported (77%) was in marriage and family relationships (Table 3). More than half of the sexual minority sample reported impairment in the areas of friendship and peer relationships (56%), sleeping habits (52%) and job/school performance (50%). Chi-square analyses found no statistically significant differences between lesbian and bisexual women in their reports of symptoms or impairment of functioning.

Substance Abuse and Suicidal Ideation. Table 4 reports frequencies for three categories of substance abuse and suicidal ideation: current ("at intake"), historical ("history of") or "ever." The third category "ever" was created to assess the presumed overlap between those who have a history of substance

TABLE 2. Frequency of Symptoms Among Lesbians and Bisexuals Seeking Mental Health Treatment

Symptom	Total Sexual Minority N = 223	Lesbian N = 191	Bisexual N = 32
Depression	190 (85.2%)	161 (84.3%)	29 (90.6%)
Anxiety	175 (78.5%)	148 (77.5%)	27 (84.4%)
Decreased Energy	119 (53.3%)	97 (50.8%)	22 (68.8%)
Grief	101 (45.3%)	85 (44.5%)	16 (50.0%)
Irritability	91 (40.8%)	74 (38.7%)	17 (53.1%)
Hopelessness	79 (35.4%)	64 (33.5%)	15 (46.9%)
Worthlessness	73 (32.7%)	58 (30.4%)	15 (46.9%)
Guilt	69 (30.9%)	56 (29.3%)	13 (40.6%)

TABLE 3. Impairment of Functioning Among Sexual Minorities Seeking Mental Health Treatment

Functioning	Total Sexual Minorities N = 223	Lesbian N = 191	Bisexual N = 32
Marriage and Family Relationships	172 (77.1%)	148 (77.5%)	24 (75%)
Friendship and Peer Relationships	125 (56%)	109 (57.1%)	16 (50%)
Sleeping Habits	115 (51.5%)	100 (52.4%)	15 (46.9%)
Job/School Performance	112 (50.2%)	97 (50.8%)	15 (46.9%)
Ability to Concentrate	95 (42.6%)	82 (42.9%)	13 (40.6%)
Financial Situation	66 (29.5%)	58 (30.4%)	8 (25.0%)
Hobbies, Interests and Play Activities	66 (29.5%)	58 (30.4%)	8 (25.0%)
Eating Habits	63 (28.3%)	51 (26.7%)	12 (37.5%)
Ability to Control Temper	59 (26.5%)	51 (26.7%)	8 (25.0%)
Sexual Functioning	38 (17.0%)	33 (17.3%)	5 (15.6%)
Physical Health	38 (17.0%)	30 (15.7%)	8 (25.0%)
Disability Leave	12 (5.4%)	12 (6.3%)	—
Activities of Daily Living	1 (.4%)	1 (.4%)	—

TABLE 4. Sexual Minorities' Experience of Substance Abuse and Suicidal Ideation

	Total Sexual Minorities N = 223	Lesbians N = 191	Bisexual N = 32
Substance Abuse (ever)	105 (47.1%)	89 (46.6%)	16 (50%)
Substance Abuse (history of)	102 (45.7%)	86 (45%)	16 (50%)
Substance Abuse (at intake)	35 (15.7%)	27 (14.1%)	8 (25.0%)
Suicidal Ideation (ever)	63 (28.3%)	53 (27.7%)	10 (31.3%)
Suicidal Ideation * (at intake)	39 (17.5%)	37 (19.7%)	2 (6.3%)
Suicidal Ideation (history of)	36 (16.1%)	27 (14.1%)	9 (28.1%)

Note. Variables with significant differences between groups are marked with asterisks (*p < .05).

abuse or suicidal ideation and those who presented with these at intake, thus capturing the overall number of sexual minorities who have experienced substance abuse or suicidal ideation in their lifetimes. Many more women reported having a history of substance abuse (46%) than reported a current problem (16%). No significant differences were found between lesbians' and bisexual women's experiences in the three categories of substance abuse. The percentage of women who reported suicidal ideation at intake (18%) was comparable to those who presented with a history of suicidal ideation (16%). Lesbians were more likely than bisexual women to present with suicidal ideation at intake (χ^2 (1) = 3.382, p = .047).

Psychiatric Diagnoses. Tables 5 and 6 list the most common Axis I and Axis IV diagnoses for lesbians and bisexual women. Because many clients are assigned more than one Axis I or Axis IV diagnosis, totals reported for each of these axes are greater than the sample size. The three most common Axis I diagnoses for both lesbian and bisexual women were adjustment disorders, mood disorders, and substance use disorders (Table 5). Although no statistically significant differences were found between the two groups with respect

TABLE 5. Axis I Diagnoses

Diagnosis	Total Sexual Minorities N = 223	Lesbian N = 191	Bisexual N = 32
Adjustment Disorders	98 (43.9%)	88 (46.1%)	10 (31.3%)
Mood Disorders	86 (38.6%)	72 (37.7%)	14 (43.8%)
Substance Use Disorders	25 (11.2%)	20 (10.5%)	5 (15.6%)
Post-Traumatic Stress Disorder	21 (9.4%)	17 (8.9%)	4 (12.5%)
Anxiety Disorders	8 (3.6%)	6 (3.1%)	2 (6.3%)
Gender Identity Disorders	6 (2.7%)	6 (3.1%)	—
Somatoform	3 (1.3%)	3 (1.5%)	—
Dissociative	1 (0.4%)	1 (.05%)	—

to any of the Axis I diagnoses, bisexual women were more commonly diagnosed with mood disorders (47% vs. 35%) and lesbians with adjustment disorders (48% vs. 28%). The most common Axis IV diagnoses for both lesbian and bisexual women included stressors related to primary support (e.g., disruptions of family circle) or social environment (e.g., inadequate social support, living alone) (Table 6). Bisexual women were significantly more likely than lesbians to present with stressors relating to social environment (χ^2 (1) = 4.456, p = .033), and health care access (χ^2 (1) = 10.826, p = .007).

DISCUSSION

Study results lend support to findings across a number of previous studies that indicate high utilization of mental health services by lesbians and bisexual women. A very large proportion of the study population (89%) had previously received some form of mental health treatment, comparable to community survey findings, wherein self-reported mental health services utilization rates have ranged from 70% to 80% (Hughes et al., 2000; Morgan, 1992; Bradford et al., 1994; Sorenson & Roberts, 1997). The finding that a majority of women

TABLE 6. Axis IV Diagnoses

	Total Sexual Minorities	Lesbian	Bisexual
	N = 223	N = 191	N = 32
Diagnosis			
Primary Support	118 (53%)	105 (55%)	13 (40.6%)
Social Environment *	57 (25.6%)	44 (23.0%)	13 (40.6%)
Educational/Occupational	43 (19.3%)	39 (20.4%)	4 (12.5%)
Housing/Economic	17 (7.6%)	15 (7.9%)	2 (6.2%)
Health Care Access *	10 (4.5%)	5 (2.6%)	5 (15.6%)
Legal	8 (3.6%)	8 (4.2%)	――

Note. Variables with significant differences between groups are marked with asterisks (p< .05).

presented at intake with symptoms of depression and concerns about relation-ships with family and friends is also consistent with reports from community sample surveys (Bradford et al., 1994; Trippet, 1994; Sorenson & Roberts, 1997).

Lesbians and bisexual women in this clinical sample reported somewhat different reasons for seeking treatment than those most often reported in com-munity surveys. Although high rates of reported suicidal ideation and sub-stance abuse have been reported in community surveys, even higher rates could have been expected in this clinical sample. However, our findings that 18% of lesbian and bisexual women reported suicidal ideation at intake and 28% have felt suicidal in their lifetime, while clinically significant, is notably less than rates reported elsewhere (Morris et al., 2001; Bradford et al., 1994). Similarly, while 46% of sexual minorities in this clinical sample reported past problems related to substance abuse, only 16% presented with current prob-lems related to substance abuse, a rate comparable to those found in commu-nity surveys of lesbians *in general* (e.g., Bradford et al., 1994; Hughes, Johnson, & Wilsnack, 2001; Sorenson & Roberts, 1997).

Although our clinical sample cannot be compared directly to community samples, this discrepancy in reported patterns of past and present substance abuse is important for service planning. Sexual minority women who seek mental health services may be less likely to acknowledge current problems with substances than they are to report past problems–a matter of direct rele-vance for service planning. Lower reported rates of substance abuse could also reflect trends in local treatment use, such that lesbians and bisexual women with substance abuse-related problems may be more likely to choose sites other than FCH. Nevertheless, chart review findings demonstrate that FCH providers cannot afford to overlook the need for substance abuse screening as a standard component of mental health service intakes.

Our findings related to symptoms, functioning and psychiatric diagnoses point to other important areas in which lesbians and bisexual women are likely to experience impairment. Taking sexual minority patients as a whole group, 85% reported feeling depressed and 78% reported feeling anxious. In addition, six of the other seven symptoms reported by nearly one-third of the sample, including decreased energy, grief, and hopelessness, are characteristic of depressive and anxiety disorders. Other studies have also found depression and anxiety to be major concerns of sexual minorities, yet rarely to the extent found here. Although one would expect the current rates of depressive symptoms found in this clinical sample to be higher than those found in community samples, they also exceed those found in clinical samples of women in general.

This sample also reported substantial impairment in their relationships. For instance, 77% reported some impairment in marriage and family relationships; 56% in friendship and peer relationships. Similarly, clinician ratings of stressors related to the clients' presenting problem indicated that more than one-half had some disruption of primary support networks, and more than one-fourth, some disruption of support in their social environments. These findings of high rates of interpersonal and social support stressors, along with the high percentages of women reporting depressive symptoms, are consistent with Oetjen and Rothblum's (2000) findings that perceived social support from friends, relationship status satisfaction, and perceived social support from family are significant predictors of depression.

Few significant differences were found between lesbians and bisexual women, who were quite similar with respect to reports of symptoms, functional impairments, substance abuse and Axis I diagnoses. Lesbians and bisexual women differed on only two measures: lesbians were more likely than bisexual women to present at intake with suicidal ideation, and bisexuals were more likely to present with stressors related to social environment and health care access. The differences should be interpreted with caution since the disproportionate sizes of the two groups may have influenced the results. These findings are quite different from those of Rothblum and Factor (2001) who found that bisexual women had significantly poorer mental health than either heterosexual women or lesbians, based on a symptom inventory commonly used in non-clinical samples. With very limited research available on the mental health needs of bisexual women, our findings illustrate the need for studies with larger and more diverse samples, to facilitate valid comparisons of lesbians and bisexual women.

Future research is needed to determine how this clinical sample is similar to women who seek mental health treatment in other settings. When study results are compared to those of past community surveys, our sample appears to be less symptomatic. Although these observed differences may not be meaningful, it is possible that they reflect broader sociopolitical changes affecting the sexual minority community. Increased recognition and acceptance of lesbians and gay men in our culture and the availability of social and health resources may have lessened the stress experienced by sexual minorities. Alternatively, the high rates of reported depressive and anxiety symptoms among this population may be related to both the high rates of historical, and low rates of current, substance abuse. That is, for some, symptoms of anxiety and depression may have become unmasked once they stopped abusing substances, resulting in higher discomfort with, and reports of, these symptoms.

Study findings concerning the relative importance of certain mental health needs are more clearly meaningful when used to inform treatment planning and prevention services for community clinical settings similar to FCH. Even if investigations in other settings reveal different *specific* concerns among its sexual minority population, this study highlights the importance of attending to environmental stressors. Treatment planning on both the individual and organizational levels must attend to the wide-ranging concerns of depression, anxiety, social isolation, and difficulties in navigating relationships. Consideration of environmental stress is important for all clients, but is predictably even more relevant for sexual minorities.

The current findings also highlight the importance of considering the full range of treatment modalities when making treatment recommendations. Although individual therapy is often very helpful for women struggling with relationship issues, group therapy may be more effective in addressing the interpersonal problems that often underlie relationship difficulties. To the extent that some of the relationship issues and/or depressive symptoms faced by sexual minorities concern coming out, both psycho-educational and psychodynamic groups would be helpful in addressing the many stages of the coming out process.

Our study found striking discrepancies between client reports of symptoms and clinicians' diagnoses of disorders, raising interesting questions about mental health assessment. Whereas 79% of all sexual minority women in this sample reported some level of anxiety, only 4% received a diagnosis of anxiety disorder. Similarly, 85% reported some level of depression, and over 45% reported decreased energy or grief–symptoms often related to depression–yet only 39% were diagnosed with a mood disorder. There are several explanations of these discrepancies. One possible explanation is that client reports of certain symptoms as documented in charts were not sufficient to warrant a clinical diagnosis. Alternatively, the process of diagnosis may be contaminated, either inflated or minimized, by managed care constraints on billing or patient concerns about confidentiality. It is also possible that there is some difference between what clients are reporting and how this information is processed by clinicians when forming a diagnosis. In any case, this discrepancy between patient reports and clinician judgments needs to be better understood. A greater reliance on standardized diagnostic tools could help to clarify the reasons for such discrepancies, by minimizing the extent to which external pressures interfere with the diagnostic process. More widespread use of standardized measures would assure greater reliability of diagnoses, improve the process of identifying clinical issues relevant to different sub-populations, improve treatment planning, and ultimately, improve clinical outcomes.

LIMITATIONS AND DIRECTIONS FOR FUTURE RESEARCH

There are several limitations to the current study. First, the study reports the mental health needs of a clinical sample, and thus, the findings do not represent and cannot be generalized to the needs of sexual minority women as a whole. Second, because study participants were patients in a specialized setting where LGBT concerns are openly acknowledged and addressed, the findings only partially represent the general population of sexual minority women who seek treatment. They represent a sub-sample of women who are more "out" and whose comfort with the identity of sexual minority may be greater than the population of sexual minorities as a whole. Given recent findings that being out as a sexual minority is negatively related to psychological distress and suicidality (Morris et al., 2001), it is possible that characteristics of this clinical sample underestimate the "true" distress of sexual minorities who seek treatment. Further, because this sample was predominately Caucasian, the findings cannot be generalized to sexual minorities of different ethnic groups.

The lack of standardized self-report measures and diagnostic tools also limits the ability to compare these findings with those from other mental health settings. Although the instruments used by this clinic have proved to have clinical utility, the absence of demonstrated validity and reliability highlights one of the most important directions for future research. Future research rooted in standardized measures for mental health assessment would greatly advance our understanding of the mental health needs of sexual minorities. Research on clinical populations using these measures would yield data that not only are less susceptible to clinician variability but also allow for comparisons across different clinical populations. Because refinement of clinical services is one of the basic purposes for examining the needs of specific clinical populations, more information is needed about sexual minorities who seek treatment from a variety of services, including those that do not specialize in LGBT care. In general, much more research is needed to better understand the mental health needs of sexual minority groups as well as barriers to accessing needed services. LGBT community health centers appear to be valuable sites in which to study and learn more about these issues, as well as potential venues for testing the efficacy of improved models of care.

REFERENCES

American Psychiatric Association. (1994). Diagnostic and statistical manual of mental disorders. Fourth edition (DSM-IV). American Psychiatric Association, Washington D.C.

Bloomfield, K. (1993). A comparison of alcohol consumption between lesbians and heterosexual women in an urban population. *Drug and Alcohol Dependency, 33,* 257-69.

Bradford, J., Ryan, C., & Rothblum, E. (1994). National Lesbian Health Care Survey: Implications for mental health care. *Journal of Consulting and Clinical Psychology, 62,* 228-242.

Bradford, J., Ryan, C., Honnold, J., & Rothblum, E. (2001). Expanding the research infrastructure for lesbian health. *American Journal of Public Health, 91*(7), 1029-1032.

Bradford, J., & White, J. (2000). Lesbian health research. In M.B. Goldman & M.C. Hatch (Eds.), *Women & Health* (pp. 64-77). San Diego: Academic Press.

Bradford, J., Rogers, T., Rice, L., & Roberts, L. (2001, June). *Expanding capacity for lesbian research in LGBT health centers: A report from the lesbian research readiness study.* National Lesbian Health Conference, San Francisco, CA.

Carroll, N., Linde, R., Mayer, K., Lara, A., & Bradford, J. (1999). Developing a lesbian health research program: Fenway Community Health Center's experience and evolution. *Journal of the Gay and Lesbian Medical Association, 3*(4), 145-152.

Clark, M.E., Landers, S., Linde, R., & Sperber, J. (2001). The GLBT Health Access Project: A state-funded effort to improve access to care. *American Journal of Public Health, 91,* 895-896.

Cochran, S.D., & Mays, V.M. (1994). Depressive distress among homosexually active African American men and women. *American Journal of Psychiatry, 151,* 524-529.

Cochran, S.D., & Mays, V.M. (2000). Relation between psychiatric syndromes and behaviorally defined sexual orientation in a sample of the US population. *American Journal of Epidemiology, 151*(5), 1-8.

Gambrill, E.A., Stein, T.J., & Brown, C.E. (1984). Social services use and need among Gay/Lesbian residents of the San Francisco Bay Area. *Journal of Social Work & Human Sexuality, 3,* 51-69.

Gay and Lesbian Medical Association. (2000). *Healthy people 2010: Companion document for lesbian, gay, bisexual and transgender (LGBT) health.* San Francisco, CA.

Herek, G.M., Gillis, J.R., & Cogen, J.C. (1999). Psychological sequelae of hate-crime victimization among lesbian, gay, and bisexual adults. *Journal of Consulting and Clinical Psychology, 67*, 945-951.

Hughes, T.L., Haas, A.P, Razzano, L., Cassidy, R., & Matthews, A.K. (2000). Comparing lesbians and heterosexual women's mental health: Results from a multi-site women's health survey. *Journal of Gay & Lesbian Social Services, 11*(1), 57-76.

Hughes, T.L., Johnson, T., & Wilsnak, S.C. (2001). Sexual assault and alcohol abuse: A comparison of lesbians and heterosexual women. *Journal of Substance Abuse.*

Mayer, K., Appelbaum, J., Rogers, T., Lo, W., Bradford, J., & Boswell, S. (2001). The evolution of the Fenway Community Health model. *American Journal of Public Health, 91*, 892-894.

McKirnan, D.J., & Peterson, P.L. (1989). Alcohol and drug use among homosexual men and women: Epidemiology and population characteristics. *Addictive Behaviors, 14*, 545-553.

Millman, M. (Ed.) (1993). *Access to health care in America.* Washington, DC: National Academy Press.

Morgan, K.S. (1992). Caucasian lesbians'use of psychotherapy: A matter of attitude. *Psychology of Women Quarterly, 16*, 127-130.

Morris, J.F., Waldo, C.R., & Rothblum, E.D. (2001). A model of predictors and outcomes of outness among lesbian and bisexual women. *American Journal of Orthopsychiatry, 71*, 61-71.

Rothblum, E.D., & Factor, R. (2001). Lesbians and their sisters as a control group: Demographic and mental health factors, *Psychological Science, 12* (1), 63-69.

Ryan, C., Bradford J., & Honnold, J. (1999). Social workers' and counselors' understanding of lesbian needs. *Journal of Gay & Lesbian Social Services, 9*(4), 1-26.

Sandfort, T.G., de Graaf, R., Bijl, R., & Schnabel, P. (2001). Same-sex sexual behavior and psychiatric disorders. *Archives of General Psychiatry, 58*, 85-91.

Scout, Bradford, J., & Fields, C. (2001). Removing the barriers: Improving practitioners' skills in providing health care to lesbians and women who partner with women. *American Journal of Public Health, 91*, 989-990.

Solarz, A. (Ed.) (1999). *Lesbian health: Current assessment and directions for the future.* Washington, DC: National Academy Press.

Sorensen, L., & Roberts, S.J. (1997). Lesbian uses of and satisfaction with mental health services: Results from Boston Lesbian Health Project. *Journal of Homosexuality, 33*, 35-49.

Trippet, S.E. (1994). Lesbians' mental health concerns. *Health Care for Women International, 15*, 317-323.

U.S. Department of Health and Human Services (2000). *Healthy people 2010: Understanding and improving health.* 2nd ed. Washington, DC: U.S. Government Printing Office.

Index